Great Medieval Projects

You Can Build Yourself

Kris Bordessa
Illustrated by Shawn Braley

Nomad Press
A division of Nomad Communications
10 9 8 7 6 5 4 3 2 1
Copyright © 2008 by Nomad Press
ISBN: 978-1-9346702-6-2

Illustrations by Shawn Braley

Questions regarding the ordering of this book should be addressed to
Independent Publishers Group
814 N. Franklin St.
Chicago, IL 60610
www.ipgbook.com

Nomad Press
2456 Christian St.
White River Junction, VT 05001

Nomad Press is committed to preserving ancient forests and natural resources. We elected to print *Great Medieval Projects* on 4,315 lb. of Rolland Enviro100 Print instead of virgin fibres paper. This reduces an ecological footprint of:

Tree(s): 37
Solid waste: 1,057kg
Water: 100,004L
Suspended particles in the water: 6.7kg
Air emissions: 2,321kg
Natural gas: 151m3

It's the equivalent of:
Tree(s): 0.8 american football field(s)
Water: a shower of 4.6 day(s)
Air emissions: emissions of 0.5 car(s) per year

Nomad Press made this paper choice because our printer, Transcontinental, is a member of Green Press Initiative, a nonprofit program dedicated to supporting authors, publishers, and suppliers in their efforts to reduce their use of fiber obtained from endangered forests.

For more information, visit www.greenpressinitiative.org

FSC
Recycled
Supporting responsible
use of forest resources

Cert no. SW-COC-000952
www.fsc.org
© 1996 Forest Stewardship Council

Other titles from Nomad Press

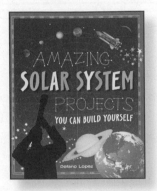

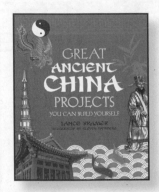

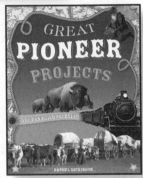

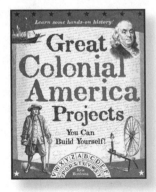

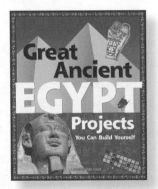

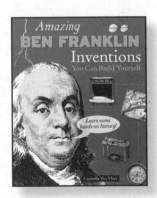

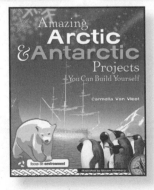

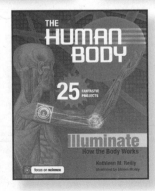

Contents

Introduction

Good morrow, my lord and my lady! Have you ever wondered what it would be like to live in a castle? Or to don a suit of armor and head out to battle on your trusty steed?

This book will help you discover what life was like in **medieval Europe**. When we think of that time, we often think of King Arthur and his Knights of the Round Table, Merlin the magician, or fire-breathing dragons. While some of this is real history, the Middle Ages is full of **myth** and **legend**, and finding out what really happened can be a difficult task!

So what was medieval Europe like? It was a time when **feudal lords** and kings ruled the land, and castles dotted the European countryside. It was also a chaotic time, as these rulers battled for control of land, culture, and religion.

But many of the people who lived during the Middle Ages were poor **peasants** or **tradesmen**. They never set foot inside a castle's grand hall. Instead, they lived in small thatched huts in villages owned by a feudal lord. Protective walls surrounded the villages, and even entire cities, because of the constant threat of war.

During this time, Christianity spread throughout Western Europe. Before the rise of Christianity, the people of Europe worshipped many gods instead of one. During the Middle Ages, kings and queens forced people to abandon these old beliefs and become Christians. Ultimately, the Christian church became very powerful. It controlled the entire political and legal system of Europe.

This book will show you how people lived, ate, and entertained themselves during the Middle Ages. You'll meet some real life medieval characters. And you will create projects that will help you learn about life in a medieval village, town, and castle.

Most of the activities in this book can be made by kids with minimal adult supervision. The supplies are either common household items or easily available at craft stores. So get ready to step back in time to medieval Europe and Build it Yourself!

Words To Know

medieval Europe: Europe during the Middle Ages, a period of time from about 350 to 1450 CE.

myth: a traditional story dealing with ancestors or heroes, or even supernatural figures.

legend: an ancient story that may or may not have really happened.

feudal lord: a member of feudal society who owned the land and had power over others.

feudal society: the social system that developed in Europe between the ninth and fifteenth centuries. Kings and barons provided land to vassals in exchange for their loyalty.

peasant: a farmer in feudal society who lived on and farmed land owned by his lord.

tradesmen: a skilled worker, such as a stonecutter or tailor.

The Making of
Medieval Europe

The medieval era, roughly during the years 350—1450, is also known as the Middle Ages. This is because the era came between the fall of the Roman Empire and the period known as the Renaissance.

The people of the Renaissance were the first ones to use the term "Middle Ages." They saw this period as a low point in history. Even though the term "Middle Ages" was originally meant to be unkind, historians still use it today.

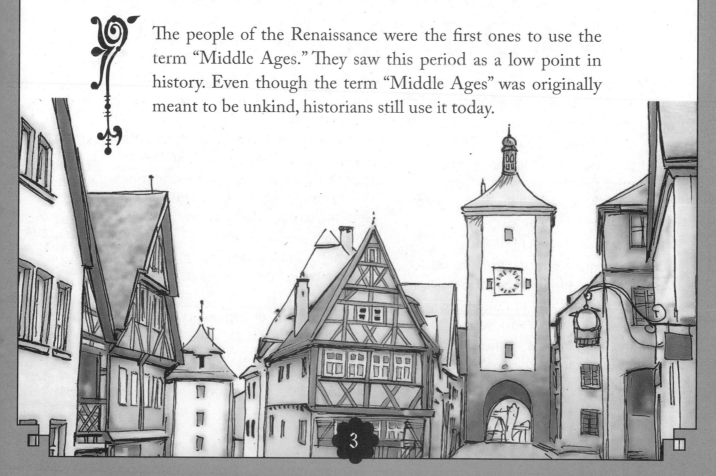

Of course, the inhabitants of the Middle Ages didn't see themselves as "between" anything. They felt—just as we do today—that the current times were as modern as they could be.

During the early Middle Ages, Europe included the islands of Britain and Ireland, along with much of the land that we now call Italy, Germany, and France. To the north were the Vikings, people who lived in the lands we now call Denmark, Norway, Sweden, and Finland. This group of countries is called Scandinavia. To the south, across the Mediterranean Sea, was Africa. The northern part of Africa was populated by Moors, who were Muslim. To the east was the **Byzantine Empire**, which included modern-day Turkey and parts of Greece, Bulgaria, and the islands of Sicily and Sardinia. Further to the east was Asia, home of the Arabians and the Huns. The people of these lands often battled with each other.

THE PEOPLE OF MEDIEVAL EUROPE

Anglo-Saxons: the people from Germanic tribes who migrated to the island of Britain.

Arabians: people from the Arabian Peninsula, which today includes Saudi Arabia.

Franks: people of German descent.

Germanic: people originating from northern Europe including Danes, Swedes, Norwegians, and Germans.

Huns: nomads from central Asia.

Magyars: people of Hungarian descent.

Moors: Muslim inhabitants of the area including present day Gibraltar, Spain and Portugal, and western Africa.

Normans: people from medieval northern France, with Scandinavian roots. "Normans" is from "Northmen" or "Norseman."

Ostrogoths: one of two main branches of the Goths, an East Germanic tribe (the Visigoths were the other).

Saracens: people who are not Christians, especially Muslims living in Arabia.

Saxons: a group of old Germanic tribes descending from northern Germany and the eastern Netherlands.

Vikings: people from the northern lands of what is now Norway, Sweden, and Finland.

Visigoths: one of two main branches of the Goths, an East Germanic tribe (the Ostrogoths were the other).

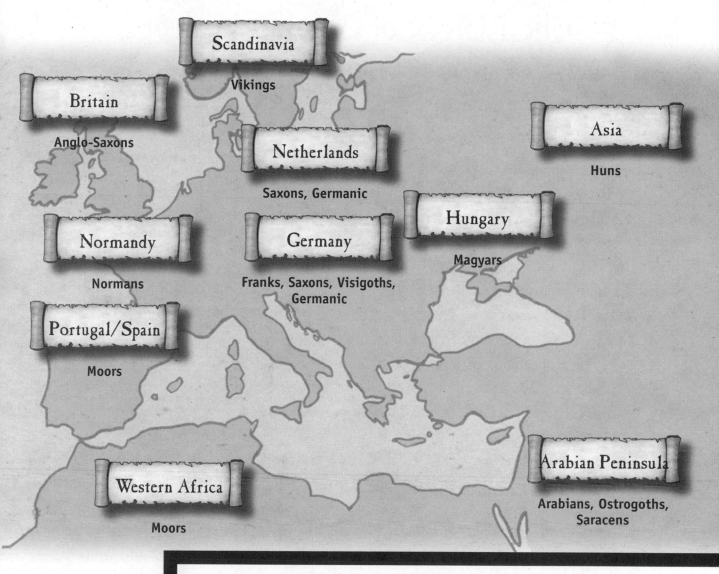

Scandinavia

Vikings

Britain

Anglo-Saxons

Asia

Huns

Netherlands

Saxons, Germanic

Normandy

Normans

Germany

Franks, Saxons, Visigoths, Germanic

Hungary

Magyars

Portugal/Spain

Moors

Western Africa

Moors

Arabian Peninsula

Arabians, Ostrogoths, Saracens

HIGHS & LOWS

Because the Middle Ages cover such a long span of time, historians have divided the era into three periods. The Early Middle Ages, often called the Dark Ages, lasted from about 350 to 1050. The High Middle Ages was from about 1050 to 1300. The Late Middle Ages was after that, ending in about 1450.

The History of Medieval Europe

The history of medieval Europe is long and complicated. In order to understand it, it's important to know a little bit about the Roman Empire, which was in power right before the Middle Ages.

Historians estimate that at the height of its glory, the Roman Empire was home to as many as 60 million people. The Roman Empire covered much of the land we now know as Europe as well as land along the northern coast of Africa and the western portion of Asia.

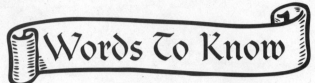

Words To Know

Byzantine Empire: a nineteenth-century term used to describe what was left of the Roman Empire during the Middle Ages.

self-sufficient: able to provide for your own needs without help from others.

barbarians: people that the Romans thought were primitive.

As the Roman Empire grew, controlling so much land and so many people became difficult. To make it easier, the Roman emperor Diocletian divided the huge empire into two parts in the third century—the West Roman Empire and the East Roman Empire. The East Roman Empire was later called the Byzantine Empire. But even though it was made smaller, the West Roman Empire struggled.

You may have heard people talk about the fall of Rome. While it sounds like a terrible tragedy that happened very quickly, it actually took hundreds of years. War and disease killed off many Romans. Large cities shrank in size and people abandoned the smaller cities. Streetlights, sewers, and running water systems fell into disrepair. Roofs fell in and pavement broke apart.

Without successful communities, people became **self-sufficient**, depending largely on themselves and on farming to survive.

The weakened state of the Roman Empire was like an invitation for surrounding tribes to attack. Some tribes wanted to settle in the lands that they attacked, but more often, armies raided for money. Raiders invaded churches and the homes of the wealthy and stole what money and jewels they could carry away on their horses. The Romans called these outsiders **barbarians** because they did not speak Rome's Latin language or live the way the Romans did. Barbarian tribes attacked the Romans over the course of hundreds of years.

WHAT'S IN A CENTURY?

People who lived during the Middle Ages didn't keep accurate records in the way we do today. In many cases, historians can't narrow a date down to a specific year, but they can identify the century. Because of this, it's important to understand what a century is. Each century is one hundred years. We count these years from the birth of Christ up to today. The first century includes the years up to 99, the second century includes the years from 100 to 199, the third century includes the years from 200 to 299, and so on.

Though Rome didn't fall on a single date, one critical event happened in the year 476. This was when the western—and smaller—half of the Roman Empire came under control of the Franks, a group of people from the north. The East Roman Empire, including the city of Constantinople, continued to thrive. Even though its empire continued to shrink and nearly disappeared during the Middle Ages, Rome was never completely removed from the map.

KING ARTHUR

King Arthur and his Knights of the Round Table are perhaps the most famous medieval characters of all—and no one knows if they were real people! The legends of King Arthur have been told for over a thousand years, and historians are still looking for clues about him.

According to legend, King Arthur ordered that a round table be built for his men to dine around so that all men—including the king—were equal as they discussed the affairs of the kingdom. A rectangular table puts at least one person at the head of the table where he appears superior.

How did this great and fair man become king? Why, he pulled a sword out of a stone, of course. Raised by a foster family, he was unaware that his father was the High King of Britain, making Arthur the heir to the throne. Merlin the Wizard knew of Arthur's rightful place as king and set a task that only young Arthur could accomplish. The magical Merlin embedded a sword in a stone and challenged men to remove the sword. The man who was able to pull the sword free should be the next king. Arthur successfully removed the sword from the stone, taking his place on Britain's throne.

King Arthur and his wife, Queen Guinevere, lived in Camelot. Many bold and brave knights traveled from afar to visit Camelot. Some of these knights remained at Camelot in service to King Arthur.

One of the most famous parts of the King Arthur legend is his knights' search for the Holy Grail. The Grail legend claims that Jesus used a vessel—a dish or goblet—that became known as the Holy Grail. People believed that the Holy Grail had miraculous powers. They believed it could provide food for those who didn't sin and would make those with impure hearts blind. A dish with such powers was very enticing, and became the subject of many quests for King Arthur and his Knights of the Round Table.

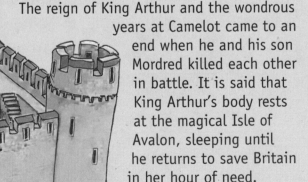

The reign of King Arthur and the wondrous years at Camelot came to an end when he and his son Mordred killed each other in battle. It is said that King Arthur's body rests at the magical Isle of Avalon, sleeping until he returns to save Britain in her hour of need.

OLD ENGLISH & ANGLO-SAXONS

Medieval Europe covered a vast amount of land and included many tribes who all spoke different languages. Numerous tribes spoke Germanic languages, including German, Dutch, English, Scandinavian languages, Afrikaans, Flemish, Frisian, and an extinct Gothic language. The people from these Germanic tribes were called Anglo-Saxons.

These people migrated to the island of Britain and over time developed a common language that we call Old English (or sometimes, Anglo-Saxon). Our own English language has roots in Old English. While Old English sounds as if we might be able to understand it, it would really be like learning an entire new language.

In the fifth century, the Romans left Britain, leaving the residents there to defend themselves. For two hundred years, the native people of Britain fought invading Scottish tribes and the Anglo-Saxons who came from the coasts of Denmark and Germany. It is during this time that a British chieftain called Arthur became famous for his exploits. Is this the man we know as King Arthur? Historians are still debating about that!

Even while so-called barbarians controlled much of the land in the area we now know as Europe, many of the Roman ways remained. Roman language, law, and religion became mixed together with the culture of the invading barbarians. Romans and barbarians also married and had children. Gradually, the differences between the two peoples grew smaller.

EXCALIBUR

There are two stories of King Arthur's sword, Excalibur. In one version, the sword Arthur pulls from the stone is Excalibur, the sword that he will use for the rest of his life. In another version, the sword is a gift from the Lady of the Lake, a mysterious woman from the magical Isle of Avalon. In both stories, Excalibur and its **scabbard** have magical properties that keep the bearer of Excalibur safe from harm.

ATTILA & THE HUNS

In 451, Mongolian Huns came out of Asia and invaded Gaul, a large area of land that includes present-day northern Italy, France, Belgium, western Switzerland, and portions of the Netherlands and Germany. The Huns were nomads, which means they wandered from place to place instead of settling down. The faces of the Huns were scarred and horrific. When they were infants, adults cut them, leaving behind gruesome scars (so that they'd grow into frightful warriors.)

A fearsome man called Attila, or the "Scourge of God," led the attack. The Romans, along with the Germanic Visigoths and other German tribes, defended Gaul. The Huns left this battleground defeated and headed on horseback for Italy. They reached the walls of Rome, where another battle ensued. But when Attila the Hun died unexpectedly, the Huns fled.

DID YOU KNOW?

Without the Internet, cell phones, or cable television, it was entirely likely that many people didn't even know of the barbarians. If a person lived off the path of the invasion, he could very easily go about daily life completely unaware of the battles happening in the distance.

The Beginning of Feudalism

The Early Middle Ages were a violent time as people fought over land or defended themselves against raiders. Feudalism developed amid this violence. Feudalism (also called the feudal system) was a social and economic system in which land was granted in exchange for military service and loyalty. The medieval feudal system centered around the king who protected his people and lands. Kings needed men to help them control their lands. These men were called **counts**. Each count had to provide a small army, enlisted from the local community. The counts gave these fighters—called knights—a portion of land. These early knights were often peasants, and some even started out as lowly serfs. Serfs were the poorest members of feudal society.

Emperors of the failing Roman Empire eventually gave land to wealthy nobles called **barons** in exchange for their loyalty. The baron owned this land—called a **manor**—and everything on it. A manor might include a big house or a castle, a village, and farmland.

The baron granted **vassals** some of this land. The land granted to a vassal was called a **fief**. The vassal farmed his fief to provide for his family, but still had to spend much of his time farming and providing food for

Words To Know

scabbard: a sheath that holds a sword.

count: a man who managed and defended land and judged local disputes.

baron: the lowest grade of nobility, barons controlled the manor and his vassals, just as lords did. However, a baron held land that had been granted directly to him by the king.

manor: area of land that the king granted to a baron.

vassal: a knight loyal to his lord.

fief: the land given to a baron or vassal.

FUNNY NAMES

In the early Middle Ages, people didn't have last names like we do today. They simply used one name. As you can imagine, this could get confusing. Later on, people were known by the name of their father, such as Charles, son of John. Over the years, this changed to Johnson. Some people used their place of birth, such as John of Paris, while others used their occupations such as Tom the Smith. Some names referred to a person's appearance or character such as Charles the Great.

Charles the Great (Charlemagne) doesn't sound like a bad name to have, right? But what if you were "short" instead of "great"? Take a look at some of the names that people had in medieval times: Charles the Simple, Charles the Fat, Louis the Stammerer, Louis the Blind, Charles the Bald, and Louis the Child.

SERFS, PEASANTS, LORDS & BARONS

Many terms for different classes of people during the Middle Ages are often interchanged, sometimes making it difficult to figure out who's who! First, you'll notice the words "noble" and "nobility" used throughout this book. Nobility is hereditary, which means passed down by birth. It refers to someone who is notable (or known) and is a part of the highest social class. Nobles are members of the nobility. They were often wealthy, but not always. Nobility was a status that was inherited or earned through exceptional service, as in the case of knights who served their master well.

Here's a quick look at how the social classes stack up.

Serfs: A member of the lowest feudal class in medieval Europe. "Serf" comes from the Latin word servus meaning slave, although serfs were not owned as slaves were. A serf was bound to land owned by someone else. Serfs had to work for, and sometimes give a portion of their crops to the land-owner. Serfs were not free to leave. They had to have permission from their lords before leaving the land.

Peasants: Living in more or less the same environment as serfs, peasants were poor villagers. But they had their freedom. Peasants were most often farmers who owned or rented their land, and could do what they wanted with it.

Villeins: Villeins were pretty much the same as serfs. But, unlike serfs, they had the same rights and freedoms as peasants in dealing with other people.

Vassals: a term used to identify the lower class, including serfs, villeins, and peasants.

Knights: A class of men who fought for and protected the lands of their Lord, Baron, Count, or King. Knights were not considered nobles during the Early Middle Ages. However, as time passed the status of knights increased and they became an important and respected part of the nobility.

Lords: Lords were the owners or managers of manors. They had authority over the vassals who worked the land.

Barons: The lowest grade of nobility, barons controlled the manor and their vassals, just as lords did. However, a baron held land that the king granted directly to him.

Counts: A man assigned by the king to oversee and manage property within the kingdom.

Kings: Male rulers who had supreme power or authority over their land.

the manor house as well. The baron also expected his vassals to fight for him or the king if need be. For his part, the baron offered protection to his vassals. If something happened to a vassal, the baron cared for the vassal's family. The feudal system would become the standard of life throughout the Middle Ages.

The knights served their king bravely during this tumultuous time. As the king became dependent upon his soldiers, they became a valuable part of a country's defenses against attack. These knights became a central part of medieval history and many were highly regarded. Knights in the king's court were not simply knights, but nobles.

Times of Change

As different rulers took control, people moved through the lands of Europe. They were often following, or fleeing from, powerful armies. The nations that were created during the Middle Ages were made up of many different people from different backgrounds. Cultures clashed, then merged, and new customs and beliefs developed.

With the government always at war, people began to depend upon the church and its **bishops** for stability. The church gradually became a strong force in medieval Europe. Everyone from kings to serfs were afraid to incur the wrath of the clergy, and therefore, God.

DID YOU KNOW?

The adjective *medieval* comes from the Latin words medium (middle) and aevum (age).

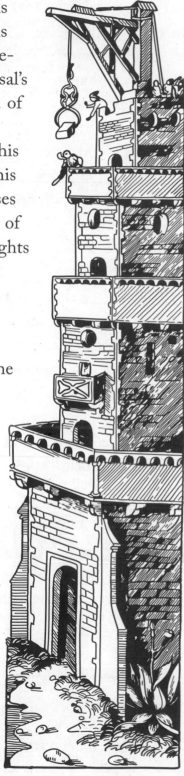

By the year 1000, the medieval world began to change somewhat, especially near larger cities. Farmers discovered that by growing crops in a different field each year—a method called crop rotation—the soil remained healthier, and crops were more suc-

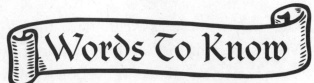
Words To Know

bishop: an important person in the church having authority over priests.

commerce: an exchange of goods.

cessful. Larger crops meant extra food, and families could afford to feed more children. The population exploded, and cities grew in size. Some peasants moved into cities—or gradually created new ones—to take advantage of the growing **commerce**. Peasants who remained in the country, however, saw little improvement in their lives.

During the High Middle Ages, kingdoms grew and wealthy rulers built the grand castles that we associate with the medieval era. The castles became a center of social life, as rulers tried to impress other nobles with their good fortune and wealth. One castle in Palermo, Sicily, had gold and silver on its floors and an artificial lake in the royal gardens.

Even with the improved situation of many of the people, Europe during the Middle Ages continued to be the site of many battles. Powerful rulers fought for control during those years between 350 and 1450, the years we now call the medieval era.

COURTLY SPEECH

If we could step back in time and listen to a medieval conversation, it would be like listening to a foreign language. However, many plays, books, and movies about medieval times use a form of speech that appeared around the sixteenth century. Here are some examples:

Hail and well met! = Hello, nice to see you!

Tarry and feast. = Stay and eat.

Whither be the privies? = Where are the restrooms?

How farest thee? = How are you?

What ails thee? = What is the matter?

What be thy trade? = What is your job?

I beg thy pardon. = Excuse me.

Fare thee well. = Goodbye.

Kings and Queens

During the Middle Ages, kings and queens governed many countries, including Spain, Germany, France, Belgium, and England.

These rulers were the supreme heads of state, called **monarchs**. This type of government is called a **monarchy**. The king was the most powerful noble in any kingdom.

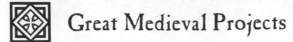

Words To Know

monarch: a supreme head of state, such as a king or queen.

monarchy: the kind of government ruled by a monarch.

alliance: an agreement between two parties to work together.

Pope: the head of the Roman Catholic church.

Normandy: a region in northern France.

census: a list that tells the king about every person and animal in the kingdom.

heir: a person who inherits a title or property from a parent.

Crown Prince: the king's first-born son, who would inherit the throne.

Kings made laws and were responsible for keeping the people of their lands safe. A strong king ruled his kingdom with honor and gained the respect of his subjects. A weak king had a hard time keeping order in his kingdom and risked being ridiculed by other nobles.

Most kings had a wife, the queen. Kings didn't marry their wives for love. Rather, they married women who would improve their kingdoms. Kings were born into high nobility and often their families chose wives for them when they were very young— even when they were just babies! If the king was an adult who still hadn't married, his choice of wife was usually a noble woman from another country. This was a great way to make an **alliance**, or political friendship.

CHARLEMAGNE
(742—814)

When a child named Charles was born to a king named Pepin the Short and his queen, big-foot Bertha, no one knew that one day he'd be known as Charlemagne. Charlemagne means "Charles the Great." That's much better than big-foot Charles, don't you think? King Pepin ruled the palace in pre-Carolingian France. After Pepin died, Charlemagne inherited the kingdom, and expanded his domain. Charlemagne wanted his kingdom to be as grand as Rome had been before its collapse, but the Romans considered him to be a barbarian. During his reign, Charlemagne built schools, worked to make education more readily available, and tried to make one language standard throughout his kingdom. The fair and kind Charlemagne was one of the greatest kings of the medieval era. In the year 800, the **Pope** named Charlemagne Holy Roman Emperor.

WILLIAM THE CONQUEROR

In 1066, William, the Duke of **Normandy**, wanted to conquer England. He succeeded, and won a famous battle called the Battle of Hastings. His successful takeover of England is called the Norman Conquest. On Christmas day in 1066, William the Conqueror was crowned King of England.

After his coronation, William ordered an inventory of England, called a **census**. He wanted to know about every person and every animal that lived in his new kingdom. The people didn't like this idea, because they knew it meant they'd be taxed for their property. The census list was known as the Domesday Book—dome means judgement.

In spite of the people's concerns, King William turned out to be good for England. He worked to create a secure environment for the people and brought order to the land. When William the Conqueror died in battle in 1087, his son ascended to the throne. After the death of Henry I, in 1135, England fell into anarchy. This word comes from a Greek word that means "having no ruler." Without a strong government people stop obeying laws and countries start to fall apart.

The children of the king and queen, called princes and princesses, were the **heirs** to the throne. The eldest son was the first in line to inherit the throne and was called the **Crown Prince**. Other sons would be princes for their entire lives, unless their older brothers died before them. Only then could they become king. It was very important for the king to have a son who would be heir to the throne. When a king died without leaving an heir, entire countries could erupt in war as nobles fought about who should become the next king.

Princesses were taught how to become a lady. A princess needed to know

NAMES OF KINGS

It can be hard to keep track of all of the different kings during the Middle Ages. Even kings from different countries often had the same name. For instance, over the course of hundreds of years, England, France, Scotland, Germany, and Saxony all had at least one King Henry.

HENRY II OF ENGLAND

In 1154, Henry II was crowned King of England. Under his rule, "Merrie England" prospered. Henry II brought common law to England. This system requires judges in courts to make decisions about a person's guilt or innocence using a **jury system**. During Henry's **reign**, the jury based their decision on common knowledge, submitting information to a judge about an alleged crime. The judge determined a person's guilt or innocence. This institution of common law was not well received by the church, which had its own method of dealing with accused criminals.

Henry married Eleanor of Aquitaine, who was from France. With this marriage, Henry II added Eleanor's land to his own, extending his rule far into France. The king and queen's third son Richard would become known as Richard the Lionheart, eventually becoming heir to the throne.

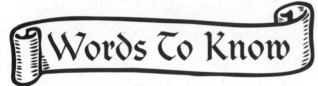

Words To Know

jury system: a court of law in which a jury, or group of citizens, decides whether the accused is innocent or guilty.

reign: the period of time that a king rules.

curtsy: a respectful gesture made by women, requiring them to bend their knees and lower their body.

court: a group of men and women who helped and supported the king and queen.

anarchy: a society without a strong government.

charter: a document that protects the king's subjects from unfair actions.

how to **curtsy** properly, embroider beautifully, and dance. A lovely princess was a bargaining tool for the king. Princesses were married to princes from other kingdoms to form an alliance between nations. A king wasn't as likely to declare war on a country where his daughter was a princess or queen.

The royal family dressed in fancy clothing. And of course, the king and queen wore golden crowns. They each had a special group of men and women who were their **court**. These people were high nobles and trusted by the king. Their clothing, while not quite as rich as that of the king and queen, was some of the fanciest in the kingdom.

The men in the king's court knew much about politics and the king depended upon them for their advice. The ladies of the queen's court were young women from noble families. These ladies kept the queen company and helped her with things like getting dressed, bathing, and combing her hair.

Everyone in the kingdom honored the king, even if they didn't agree with him. They knew that speaking out against the king, or not following his rules, could lead to big trouble. It was against the law to disagree.

DID YOU KNOW?

For about three hundred years, following the Norman conquest of England, the English royalty spoke French!

MAGNA CARTA AND KING JOHN

When Richard the Lionheart died in 1199, his younger brother John was crowned King of England. Many of King John's subjects hated him. They were angry about high taxes. They were angry when he lost much of his land to France. Some think that King John had his nephew Arthur—who ruled Brittany at the time—murdered, and they were angry about that too.

In 1215 a group of barons asked the king for a **charter**, a document that would protect everyone from King John's unfair actions. The barons armed themselves and captured the city of London to show how serious they were. The king stamped his seal of approval on a document known as the "Articles of the Barons" and the barons renewed their allegiance to the king. This document was later expanded and became the famous Magna Carta. This is Latin for "the Great Charter."

Magna Carta is a series of documents that forced the king to obey certain laws regarding the treatment of church officials and nobles. One important clause created a committee of 25 barons who could overrule the king. Before that, the king could do anything he wanted to do.

Jesters and Fools

Most people in the Middle Ages had to be careful not to offend the king or queen. Subjects couldn't criticize or speak out against their rulers because they could be severely punished—or even put to death!

The exception to the rule was the **court jester**, or fool. He alone had the ability to say bold things about the king and queen, often right in front of them. The only rule? Whatever the jester said must be a jest, or joke. Because of his ability to make the truth funny, he got away with saying things that most people couldn't.

The jester's job was to make fun of things and entertain people. He did so by dancing, juggling, clowning, and telling jokes and riddles. The jester was a celebrity. People loved to watch him and hear what he'd say next. His jokes were sometimes crude, but always made his audience laugh.

Jesters wore brightly colored clothing that was often mismatched. This made jesters highly visible in crowded courts and at medieval feasts. The most recognizable feature of the jester's costume was his hat. It had three points, with a bell at the end of each point.

Traveling **bards**, or musicians, also entertained the court. A bard usually sang his stories in verse. His songs told of events that happened in far-off places. In a world without TVs or computers, the bard provided information about what was going on in the world. Of course, he often exaggerated his stories to make them more interesting. Because of this, people had to be careful about what they believed.

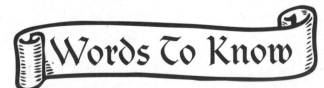

Words To Know

court jester: the court's official entertainer.

bard: a traveling musician.

Make Your Own Jester Hat

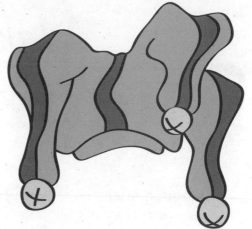

Supplies

flexible tape measure	brass fasteners
pencil	pushpin
3 pieces of craft foam, approximately 8 by 18 inches	glue
	jingle bells
	ribbon

1 Measure around your head just above your eyes. If you don't have a flexible tape measure, you can wrap a length of string around your head and then measure it with a ruler. If your measurement is 21 inches or less, use these instructions and measurements. If your head is bigger, you'll need to adjust the size of the craft foam pieces to fit your head.

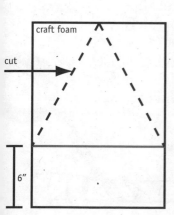

2 Draw a line 6 inches from the narrow end of each piece of craft foam. Starting where the line meets each edge, cut the opposite end of the foam pieces into a point. Each piece will have one point.

3 Join the three pieces of craft foam together by overlapping the pieces at the 6-inch sides and

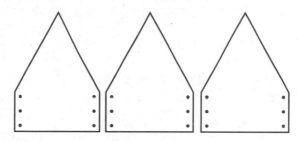

securing them together using several brass fasteners (use a pushpin to make holes for the brass fasteners). Bring the unsecured ends together and fasten in the same manner, matching the size of the hat to your head (if the hat feels too loose make adjustments when you secure the ends together).

4 For the final touch, glue a jingle bell at the tip of each point and decorate the hat with ribbon.

Make Your Own
Juggling Sticks

Juggling sticks have been around for thousands of years, but no one is quite sure how they made their way to Europe. Some people believe that they may have come to Europe from China (where they were called Devil sticks) along the Silk Road with Marco Polo. The Silk Road was an ancient trade route between China and the Mediterranean Sea. Marco Polo was a merchant and adventurer from Venice, Italy, who traveled the Silk Road in the thirteenth century. He wrote a famous book about his travels.

1 Wrap duct tape around each end of the longest dowel numerous times to create a thick "knob" on each end. This is your juggler. Do your best to keep the duct tape equal thicknesses at each end, so that the weight of the stick will be balanced. Check this by balancing the center of the stick on your finger.

DID YOU KNOW?
During the Middle Ages, doctors sometimes prescribed a dose of the court jester to sick patients. They truly believed that laughter is the best medicine!

2 Starting at the middle of the juggler, wrap electrical tape all the way to the end completely covering the stick and the duct tape knob. Repeat for other end of stick. If you'd like, add a colorful candy-cane stripe by adding a second color of electrical tape.

Supplies

duct tape

one ⅝-inch wooden dowel, 24-inches long

colored electrical tape (use more than one color for a really bright look)

two ⅜-inch wooden dowels, 18-inches long

scissors

3 pieces of felt, 4-inches by 10-inches in colors that match the electrical tape

tacky glue

3 With scissors, cut the felt pieces into a fringe by snipping 2-inch cuts into one of the long edges of each piece. Stack the felt pieces and cut them in half to make six 4-inch-by-5-inch pieces. You'll use a stack of three for each end of your juggler. Wrap the uncut long edges around the duct tape knob, gluing in place as you go so that the fringe hangs over the edge of the dowel.

4 To make the hand sticks, cover both 18-inch dowels with electrical tape.

5 To use the sticks, kneel on the floor and stand the juggler upright in front of you. Use the hand sticks to lean the juggler back and forth, making sure that one end stays on the ground. Let the weight of the juggler land on each hand stick, then use the stick to push the juggler back in the opposite direction.

Use flowing motions to try lifting the juggler off the ground a bit with each toss. It takes lots of practice, but once you have this mastered you can try all sorts of tricks with your juggling sticks. If you have access to the Internet, you can search to find movies of some really talented jugglers.

Knights and Armor

There was constant upheaval in medieval Europe. Wars, especially over religion, were common. Knights served their king bravely during this tumultuous time. As the king became dependent upon these soldiers, they became a valuable part of a country's defenses against attack. These knights are a central part of medieval history.

When people think of medieval knights, the picture that often comes to mind is an honorable knight in shining armor on a grand horse. This isn't entirely accurate. During the early part of the medieval era, knights were simply common men who were fulfilling an obligation. Sometimes these men went into battle armed with only farm tools such as hoes and shovels!

By the early eleventh century, kings began to use **cavalry**, or soldiers on horseback. With the introduction of stirrups, it became much easier for knights to stay in the saddle while using weapons. A knight on horseback was a powerful force. Armored knights could form a line, level their spears, and run down the enemy. This was called a cavalry charge. The cavalry charge soon became the most important weapon a king could use, and mounted knights became the most important soldiers on the battlefield. They also grew more important in society as well. In fact, many of them became part of the nobility. Eventually the law required all knights in training to be sons of knights.

It took years of training for a boy to achieve the status of knight. As a young child, he had to learn to be courteous and behave properly. By the time the boy reached the age of four or five, he had his own pony to ride and care for, and he spent a good amount of time in the stables, where he learned all about horses.

At the age of seven or eight, the boy was sent away to live with another well-respected family where he received further training. At this stage, he became a **page** and acted as a knight's apprentice. The page continued to learn about proper behavior and practice his horsemanship skills. Some pages even learned to read. In addition to his studies, the page helped with household chores and waited upon his lord at mealtime.

DID YOU KNOW?

The English word *knight* actually comes from an Anglo-Saxon word for servant.

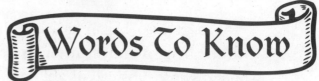

Words To Know

cavalry: soldiers on horseback.
page: a young boy who acted as a knight's apprentice.

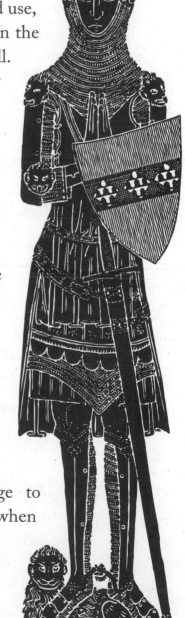

The lord and the lady of the house expected the page to appear quickly when he was called.

The page also began to learn the basics of swordsmanship with the help of an instructor. For safety reasons, pages used wooden swords instead of real ones. Even so, the instructor's sword could leave bruises if the page missed a stroke.

Once he could use his sword, the page began hunting. Coming face to face with dangerous animals such as wild boars taught him to think quickly and defend himself—a skill that would be very important in future battles.

At the age of fourteen, a page became a **squire** and was apprenticed to a knight who lived in the lord's home. The squire had many duties. He dressed his master in the morning and prepared him for bed. He helped the knight into his armor and was responsible for cleaning it after each use.

At mealtimes, he served his master and even cut the knight's meat for him.

It was also a time of hard training. The squire wrestled, jumped, and ran to build his strength for battle. He worked on improving his swordsmanship. It was important that he could wield his weapons for long periods of time without getting tired. When the squire became skilled enough in managing his weapons, he began doing practice fights with other squires.

Squires also learned the knights' code of conduct, called **chivalry**, which became popular during the High Middle Ages. Chivalry required a knight to be brave as well as honorable and loyal. He had to match his lord's courage on the battlefield and continue to fight until his lord ordered a retreat. A knight had to always obey his lord, keep his word, and never betray the trust of his lord in any matter.

STIRRUPS

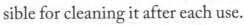

Stirrups are loops or rings that hang from either side of a horse's saddle. They support the rider's feet and make it much easier to control the horse. The stirrup probably wasn't introduced to Europe until the eighth or ninth century. The first record we have of the stirrup in Europe is a picture on an altarpiece showing a rider with stirrups. Before that, riders used only the power of their legs to remain mounted.

THE CHIVALRIC CODE

During the latter part of the Middle Ages, knights became part of the upper social class and were expected to follow a certain code of behavior. This was called chivalry. It meant that knights should follow rules of etiquette and act like true gentlemen. You might think that this was only necessary when a knight was interacting with a lady, but that's not so. Knights had to be brave in the face of danger, be honest in all things, and be loyal to their masters.

Chivalrous knights treated other knights (friend and foe) and people of lower classes with respect and courtesy, even on the battlefield. A chivalrous knight would not attack an unarmed man and he would never dream of attacking another soldier who was unprepared for battle. Many knights even thought that archers were weak soldiers, because they attacked with bow and arrows from a distance.

There were many books written telling knights how to behave properly. But there were also many different opinions about chivalry. You can be sure though, that even for kind and well-taught knights, it wasn't always easy to act appropriately all of the time!

It is believed that the foundations of chivalry came from the chaos of armies taking advantage of the weak who weren't protected by the king.

Strong, armed men stole from, killed, and tortured the poor and the weak. In the midst of this confusion, some nobles likely decided to take action to help these people by defending them. The church happily sanctioned such good works, further helping to spread the spirit of chivalry. Chivalrous knights lived by the moral virtues taught by the church, becoming trustworthy and honored in the eyes of the community. Of course, most knights wanted to be seen as honorable and trustworthy, so they followed the lead of those nobles and chivalry became an important aspect of knighthood.

Before a squire could become a knight, he had to prove that he had the skills to fulfill the job. Not every squire became a knight. Some lacked the skills necessary for knighthood. Others did

Words To Know

squire: a young man of fourteen who successfully finished his training as a page.

chivalry: a knight's code of conduct.

FANCY SWORDS

Knights often engraved their swords with a prayer or their name, and some knights had elaborately decorated, jewel-encrusted swords.

not have the land or money necessary for maintaining the lifestyle of a knight. These men remained squires, often hiring themselves out to knights.

A squire who was fit to become a knight prepared for a grand ceremony known as **dubbing**. The ceremony often took place at a great castle or even the king's residence. On the day before the ceremony, the squire confessed his sins (a knight had to be a good Christian). He cut his hair short and bathed. In the evening he dressed in a red tunic or robe, which symbolized that he was prepared to shed his blood. Finally, he prayed, always remembering that his weapons were only for use in the service of God.

After a church service, the squire faced a crowd of nobles, knights, and family members. The senior knight then delivered an **accolade**. The accolade was an openhanded blow to the neck or head, or a light sword touch to his shoulder. With this, the squire became a knight and was ready for battle.

A Knight's Weapons

Both mounted knights and foot soldiers fought their battles in hand-to-hand combat. A knight depended heavily on two weapons: his sword and his **lance**.

Lances were long, straight, wooden spears that allowed mounted men to reach their enemies from horseback. A metal tip on the end of the lance made it more dangerous. Lances were nine to fourteen feet long and were hard to handle because they were so big. To help knights balance the lance, armor was equipped with a special metal piece that helped the knight keep the lance in place. In the latter part of the Middle Ages, a round disc of iron called a **vamplate** was added to the lance.

dubbing: the act of making a squire a knight.

accolade: an open-handed blow to the neck or head, or a light sword touch to the shoulder.

lance: a long, straight wooden spear.

vamplate: a round disc of iron mounted to a lance which protected the knight's arm and hand.

shaffron: a piece of armor meant to protect a horse's head.

The vamplate protected the knight's hand and arm from damage. Charging forward, a knight aimed the tip of his lance at his opponent in hopes of knocking him from his horse. Off the horse a knight gave up the unwieldy lance in favor of his sword.

Swords were double edged. This meant that both sides of the blade could cause injury. They were expensive to make, so only the wealthiest soldiers could afford them. Knights used these swords with a slashing motion, hitting their

opponents with the sharpened edges. Archaeologists have discovered old damaged bones that show just how much damage a swinging, double-edged sword could inflict.

In the latter part of the Medieval era, plate armor replaced chain mail, making it harder for knights to inflict wounds with the edge of the blade. So knights began to carry swords with pointed tips. Thrust with great force, these swords could pierce plate armor and take down an enemy.

A knight could use other weapons as well. A battle-axe was a metal blade attached to a wooden handle. With a sharp axe on one side and a pointed tip on the other, this

WAR HORSES

While it was uncommon, some knights outfitted their war horse with plate armor. It was expensive, so if a knight could only afford partial armor, he would choose to protect the horse's head with a piece of armor called a **shaffron**.

DID YOU KNOW?

Squires used a *quintain* to practice their skills with a lance, or steel-tipped spear. A quintain was a dummy with a shield that was suspended from a pole. As the squire attacked the quintain, it spun, rotating its arms, which could knock the squire from the saddle. By avoiding the arms of the quintain, the squire learned the maneuvering skills needed in battle.

weapon could cause severe injury when a knight on horseback swung it at an enemy.

Knights also used clubs and **flails**. Clubs were topped with metal caps that could cause more injury than a plain wooden club. Flails were for foot soldiers. These fearsome weapons had an iron ball (sometimes spiked) attached to a wooden handle with a length of chain. Knights swung the flail around, putting the ball in motion, and then struck their enemies.

Soldiers also carried daggers, or short knives, as well. Because daggers were so small, soldiers only used them in very close hand-to-hand combat.

Armor

In the early Middle Ages, the protective gear that knights wore was simple. They wore a helmet and a **hauberk**, which was a thigh-length mail shirt with elbow-length sleeves. Those were the only two things between a knight and an attacking sword.

Mail was made from small metal rings that were linked together to form a sheet of woven iron. A mail shirt had about 250,000 rings and could weigh as much as 25 pounds. By the twelfth century, the hauberk had full-length sleeves with attached mail mittens. Knights also wore a mail hood and mail **chausses** to protect the legs.

The mail was flexible, which meant that while a heavy blow might not penetrate the mail, it could cause broken bones. Knights wore a heavily padded shirt under the mail to help soften blows.

While the ancient Greeks and Romans used plate armor, it fell out of favor after the fall of Rome. However, by the early thirteenth century, plate armor once again became the standard. You might think that moving around in a suit of armor would be very difficult, but that was not so. Each knight had plate armor constructed to fit him perfectly. The pieces were made as light as possible while still providing the necessary protection. The armor had to weigh less than 65 pounds in order for the knight to mount his horse and move freely in battle.

Tournament armor was twice as heavy as battle armor. In a **tournament**, or competition, knights used their lances to try to knock an opponent off his horse. Mobility wasn't as much of a concern, and the heavy armor protected the knights from injury.

Knights were proud of their armor. Wealthy knights suited up in armor that was both protective and fashionable. Their armor featured fancy details like pleating, gold plating, and engravings.

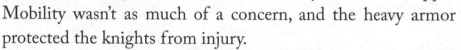 Words To Know

quintain: a dummy used by knights in practice.

flail: a weapon with an iron ball attached to a wooden handle with a length of chain.

hauberk: a thigh-length mail shirt with elbow-length sleeves.

chausses: mail to protect the legs.

tournament: a competition where knights used their lances to try to knock an opponent off his horse.

MEDIEVAL TOURNAMENTS

A tournament offered battle practice for knights, and they traveled near and far to attend. At these events, teams of mounted knights lined up, facing each other. At the sound of the bugle, both teams charged with their lances leveled at their opponents. Those who remained seated on their horse after the first charge turned quickly, seeking out an individual knight to attack.

Jousts were another popular tournament event. In these, individual knights squared off against each other, again trying to unseat their opponent. These tournaments were a friendly competition—much like football is today—and a chance for knights to showcase their talents.

Tournaments also served as entertainment. Spectators loved to watch the competitions, sometimes betting on their favorite. Following the long tournament day there was a banquet and entertainment, where prizes were awarded to the winners.

Military Religious Orders

Early in the twelfth century, organizations of medieval knights developed, these organizations performed military, religious and charitable acts. Strict vows of poverty and obedience bound the members of these orders. Three of the most famous orders were the Knights Templar (or Poor Knights of Christ); the Knights of Saint John of Jerusalem, or Hospitalers; and the Teutonic Knights of Saint Mary's Hospital at Jerusalem, or the Teutonic Knights. All three of these orders were founded in the Holy Land of Jerusalem and held a major role in defending the new Christian states that developed following the First Crusade. The First Crusade was a march to free the sacred city of Jerusalem from Muslim control (you'll read more about the Crusades later).

The Knights Templar followed rules that mimicked those of the monastery, a religious community of monks and nuns, outlining a simple religious life and requiring the knights to spend part of each day in prayer. The grand master was the leader of the order. He presided over three ranks of members: knights, chaplains and sergeants. Knights were the highest-ranking member and the only

A POOR MAN'S ARMY

During many battles, peasants mobilized to serve their baron or the king. These men were farmers, not professional soldiers. The weapons they brought to the battlefield were the same tools that they used to tend their fields: hayforks, flails, sickles, and axes. These weapons were not as glamorous as swords and lances, but they did the job. Eventually, these "farm tools" became part of the army's weapon inventory.

members allowed to wear the distinctive white tunic with a red Latin cross on the back. The grand master was responsible only to the Pope and the Knights Templar were free from the control of kings and bishops.

Originally, the Knights Templar provided military escorts to religious pilgrims on their way to Jerusalem. As the order became more successful, they developed into a strong band of knights. Through contributions from the church and other monetary favors, the Knights Templar became quite wealthy. In order to move money between their various posts, they developed a complex banking system. The Knights Templar were strong enough to safely move money for other people as well, and soon kings, nobles, and merchants came to count on them for this service, too.

In 1312 amid accusations that the knights performed religious acts forbidden by the church, King Phillip the Fair of France suppressed the organization. Under torture, the knights confessed to devil worship and blasphemy. Most of these knights were burned for **heresy**.

ROBIN HOOD

The legendary Robin Hood robbed from the rich to give to the poor. Some people might see that as chivalrous—except for the stealing part! Robin Hood wasn't a real person as far as we know, though the term Robin Hood (in medieval times, 'Robehod' or 'Hobbehod') seems to have been used to describe any outlaw.

Robin Hood and his Merry Men are the subject of numerous folk tales set in the Middle Ages. Many of the stories include real people, like Richard the Lionheart and his brother, King John. The first known Robin Hood text dates to the mid-fifteenth century, but stories of Robin Hood are still popular today.

Heraldry

A well-outfitted knight never left home without his shield. Shields protected a knight in battle, but also served another purpose. Head-to-toe armor made it difficult to distinguish friend from foe. In the twelfth century, knights began decorating their shields with identifying symbols.

The practice of decorating shields soon developed into a complex system known as **heraldry**. The colors, patterns, and symbols used on a shield each had a very specific meaning and were often called the knight's **coat of arms**. Combined, these elements told the knight's story, and every coat of arms was as unique as a fingerprint. Coats of arms became a way to identify knights on the battlefield. They could also be a status symbol, especially if a knight came from a powerful family.

Words To Know

heresy: having a belief that is not approved of by the church.

heraldry: the practice of decorating shields.

coat of arms: the colors, patterns, and symbols used on a shield.

tincture: the background, or field, of a shield.

cadency mark: a symbol to indicate a knight's place within his family.

HERALDIC COLORS

Gold: Generosity and elevation of the mind

Silver or White: Peace and sincerity

Red: Warrior or martyr, military strength and magnanimity

Blue: Truth and loyalty

Green: Hope, joy, and loyalty in love

Black: Constancy or grief

Purple: Royal majesty, sovereignty, and justice

Orange: Worthy ambition

Maroon: Patient in battle, yet victorious

The background, or field, of the shield was the **tincture**. Tinctures were of solid colors or patterned to indicate fur. Furs were marks of dignity. Shields could have many fields. Lines divided shields into halves, quarters, or even more pieces. These lines could run horizontally, vertically, or diagonally and could be simple or detailed. Each field showed a heraldic symbol that held meaning for the knight. It could be his father's crest, a symbol of his honor or faith, or a **cadency mark**. Cadency marks were a way for knights to indicate their birth order within a family. This was so people viewing the shield could identify different members of the same family.

A knight also put his coat of arms on large flags or banners. In the confusion of battle, a flag flying high on a wooden pole helped troops to rally together. When flags were not in use, knights displayed them at their home castles.

When knights traveled, they flew their flags so that people could see who was coming. Once they arrived at a castle, attendants mounted their flags on the castle so that people could identify who was visiting.

Make Your Own Shield

1 Sketch out a heraldic design of your own onto the cardboard. Use the cadency marks shown here and the heraldic symbols on page 39 as inspiration. Are you a second son or daughter? Then use the crescent. During the Middle Ages, daughters would not have carried a shield, but don't let that stop you! Are you brave? Then add a boar.

2 Once you are happy with your layout, use the paints to complete the design.

3 Hang your shield on your bedroom door to announce just who you are.

Supplies

heavy piece of cardboard cut into the shape of a shield

pencil

paints

paintbrush

CADENCY MARKS

 eldest son (during his father's lifetime) label

 fourth son martlet

 seventh son rose

 second son crescent

 fifth son annulet

 eighth son cross moline

 third son molet

 sixth son fleur-de-lis

 ninth son octofoil or double quatrefoil

Make Your Own
Mail

Note: Adult supervision is recommended for this activity.

1 Cut a length of wire about 2 feet long. Starting at one end, wrap the wire in a tight spiral around the bolt. When you reach the end of the bolt or run out of wire, slide it from the bolt. You will have a wire coil.

2 Use the wire cutters to snip in a straight line the length of the wire coil you made. This will leave you with a bunch of little metal rings that are all the same size and not quite closed.

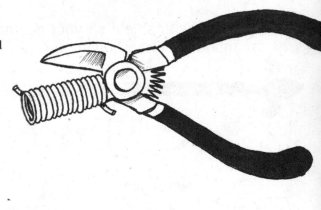

3 Use a pair of pliers in each hand to bend about half of the rings into a completely closed ring by bringing the ends together as tightly as possible. Leave the other half of the rings as they are.

4 You'll start by making lots of four-in-one links. To do this, slide four closed rings onto an open ring and then pinch the open ring closed with pliers.

5 Once you have a good collection of four-in-one links, you can connect them to make a chain. You'll use one open ring to connect two sets together. To do so, slide two rings from each set onto the open ring. Make sure to assemble the rings so that they will lie flat. Continue connecting sets until your chain is long enough for a bracelet, or if you're really inspired, keep linking.

6 To turn your chain into a larger sheet of mail, set two chain lengths side by side and connect them together with open rings.

Supplies

14 gauge baling wire, available at most hardware stores

5/16 bolt, 6 inches long

2 pairs of pliers

wire cutters

HERALDIC SYMBOLS

Acorn: Antiquity and strength

Apple: Liberality, felicity, and peace

Battle Axe: Execution of military duty

Bear: Strength, cunning, ferocity in the protection of one's kindred

Bee: Efficient industry

Boar: Bravery, fights to the death

Candle: Light, life, and spirituality

Compass: Direction

Drum: Ready for war

Fox: One who will use all that one may possess of wisdom and wit in one's own defense

Gavel: Justice, legal authority

Griffin (head, wings, and talons of an eagle with the body of a lion): Valor and death-defying bravery, vigilance

Lightning Bolt: Swiftness and power

Lion: Dauntless courage

Musical Pipes: Festivity and rejoicing

Palm Tree: Righteousness resurrection, victory

Plant: Hope and joy

Rainbow: Good times after bad

Salamander: Protection

Sun: Glory and splendor, fountain of life

Wheel: Fortune, cycle of life

Wreath of Laurel Leaves and Berries: Triumph

Make Your Own Helmet

This is a fun project but one word of caution: it is very important that you never put plaster down the drain. It will clog your plumbing.

1 This project takes two people. You will make helmets for each other that will be custom fit to each head. Decide who will be the first to sit for a helmet fitting.

2 Set up a work area. This is a messy project, so you'll need to wear old clothes and be sure to cover the floor completely with newspaper. Better yet, do this outside.

3 Cut holes in the garbage bag for your arms and head. Put the garbage bag on your friend to protect his clothes.

4 Tear two, 20-inch lengths of aluminum foil. Set one piece of foil on your friend's head. Put the second piece over this in the opposite direction. Mold these to fit around and cover your friend's head. Wrap masking tape around the foil to hold it in place. Roll up the foil edges a bit—this will help catch any drips.

5 Add a layer of plastic wrap over the foil, securing it in place with masking tape. Be certain NOT to cover anyone's face with plastic wrap.

6 In the foil pan, mix about a cup of plaster of Paris with enough water to make a mixture that is the consistency of runny yogurt. You'll need to make more as you use this mixture, but you don't want to make too much at once.

7 Now you're ready to make the helmet! Dip a strip of cloth into the plaster mixture until it's coated. Use your fingers to scrape off the excess plaster of Paris and lay the strip over the top of the plastic wrap. Keep adding strips, overlapping them until your friend's head is completely covered in several layers of cloth strips. The edges of your helmet will be a bit ragged looking. To fix this, trim off any really long pieces with scissors, then add a few strips of cloth right along the edge to make it even.

8 Now, scoop some of the plaster mixture up with your hands and smooth it over the strips to hide the fabric. Make sure you cover the entire helmet. When you are happy with the finished surface, wash your hands in the bucket of water (NOT in the sink—the plaster will clog the plumbing). Let the bucket of water sit, so the plaster settles to the bottom. Carefully pour the clear water outside, then use a paper towel or newspaper to wipe out the remaining plaster.

9 When the helmet feels like it's starting to harden, lift it off your friend's head carefully and set it on newspaper. Double check the edges. If they're rough, smooth on more strips of cloth so that they fold over the edge to the inside of the helmet. Be careful not to push the helmet out of shape. Allow to dry overnight.

10 Once the helmet is dry, use the shoe polish (for a leather look) or spray paint (for a metallic finish) to complete your helmet.

Variation: Some helmets had spikes to help deflect a sword's blow. To add spikes to your helmet, roll pieces of cardstock into cone shapes and tape them in place on the plastic wrap, before you start using the plaster of Paris. When you add the cloth strips, simply make sure that you cover the spikes.

Supplies

newspaper	plastic spoon
large garbage bag for each helmet	2 to 3 yards of cloth torn into strips 1 to 2 inches wide and about 15 inches long
aluminum foil	
masking tape	scissors
plastic wrap	bucket of water
two large foil pans	brown shoe polish or metallic spray paint
plaster of Paris	

Medieval **Warfare**

If an attacking army wanted to take over the lands of another king, they first had to take control of the king's castle. The castle was like a fortress, and attacking it required a lot of hard work and preparation.

The outer walls of a castle were called **curtain walls**. These were meant to discourage and repel attacks. Early curtain walls were made of timber and called **palisades**. These walls, though sturdy, could rot or catch fire. Stone curtain walls eventually replaced the wooden palisades. Stone curtain walls were massive, ranging from seven to twenty feet in thickness, and were about thirty feet high. A few castles even had curtain walls as tall as forty feet. Richmond Castle in North Yorkshire, England, has one of the earliest stone curtain walls, built in 1075.

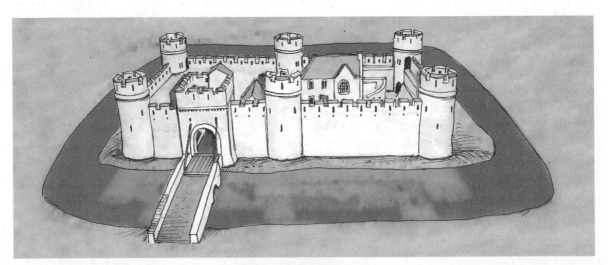

An attacking army would often put a castle under **siege**. This meant that they would surround it, preventing the occupants from escaping or coming out for provisions like food and water. While holding a castle under siege, armies would spend their time devising ways to attack the castle.

Armies used a number of different methods to **breach** the castle walls. One simple solution was a ladder. Soldiers positioned ladders so that men could climb up to the top of the castle walls. The trouble with ladders is that while a man was climbing, he was open to an attack from above. Because of this, armies built special siege weapons to help them

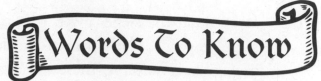

breach the walls of the castle. These weapons were huge, requiring thousands of men just to move them!

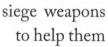

Wooden **siege towers** could be nearly one hundred feet tall. Archers hid inside the tower while other soldiers wheeled the tower into place near the castle wall. Once in place, the hidden men lowered a drawbridge onto the castle wall and emerged. They battled the defending troops on the castle walls and rained arrows down into the walled complex.

Soldiers built these massive towers right there, just outside the castle walls. This wasn't a very secretive operation, so the people inside the castle knew that an attack was coming. The castle's defenders did their best to interrupt the building of the tower. They launched fire arrows or firepots at the siege tower. To protect the siege tower, soldiers draped the hides of mules or oxen over it. These didn't catch fire as easily as the wood.

Attackers also used giant catapults called **trebuchets** to fling large, dangerous objects at the castle. Trebuchets had a moveable arm with a sling at one end and a heavy weight at the other end. When the weight dropped, the arm launched the missile in the sling. These missiles could travel hundreds of yards!

Four-hundred-pound boulders were good for knocking down castle walls. Soldiers launched other items as well, including disease-infected dead bodies that could make the people in the castle sick. They also flung the severed heads of enemy soldiers or messengers that the attackers had killed.

A **battering ram** was another important siege weapon. Soldiers built a wooden shed and used chains to hang a tree trunk horizontally from the heavy beams of the structure. They carved the end of the tree trunk into a point and capped it with iron. Then the soldiers pushed the shed close to the walls of the castle and swung the battering ram back and forth, banging the iron end into the door or wall repeatedly. The shed protected the men from the arrows that rained down on them. The attackers hoped that, eventually, the door or wall would weaken and crumble, allowing soldiers to enter into the castle.

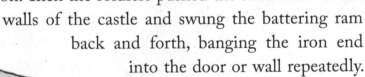
DID YOU KNOW?
There was one medieval cannon that used square ammunition!

CANNONS

You might be surprised to hear that cannons were in use during some medieval battles. While historians aren't exactly sure when the first cannon was used, documents written during the early fourteenth century mention the use of cannons. Cannons were desirable siege weapons because the strength of the blast could knock down heavy castle walls. Cannonballs were round and made of iron, lead, or even rock.

The castle's defenders did all they could to disable the battering ram. They used fire arrows to try to burn the shed and dropped mattresses in front of the battering ram to cushion the blows. They even used grappling hooks on a chain to try to catch and stop the battering ram.

Another very important weapon, though not very exciting, was simply a shovel. Soldiers used shovels to dig tunnels beneath the castle walls. While they were digging they used heavy timbers to support the castle walls, to prevent the wall from collapsing on them. Sometimes the attacking army tunneled all the way into the castle and launched a surprise attack. More often, they would simply light the wooden support timbers on fire. When they burned through, the timbers would collapse along with the castle walls.

The people who lived inside the castle walls knew that someone might tunnel in. They put bowls full of water near the castle walls. Ripples in the water showed that attackers were on the move.

Words To Know

firepot: clay pot filled with a flaming liquid like tar used to attack a castle during a siege.

trebuchet: a large, catapult-like structure with a moveable arm that launched damaging items into or over castle walls.

battering ram: a covered structure with a large, horizontal log hanging from it. Soldiers repeatedly swung the log against a castle's wall or door.

Make Your Own
Trebuchet

Note: Adult supervision is recommended for this activity.

Supplies

6 pieces of wood approximately 12 inches long and 1 to 2 inches wide

hammer and small nails

wood glue

masking tape

ruler

wooden dowel ⅝ inch or smaller in diameter, 18 inches long

drill with a bit one size larger than the diameter of the dowel rod

piece of wood approximately 8 inches long and 1 to 2 inches wide

¼ inch drill bit

empty tuna can or similarly sized tin can

pint-size milk carton

scissors

twist tie—plastic ones for trash bags work great

duct tape

weights and projectiles such as small stones, pennies, washers, marbles

1 To build your frame, nail four of the 12-inch pieces of scrap wood together to form a square, adding wood glue to the joints for extra stability.

2 Use the masking tape to secure the last two 12-inch pieces of wood together. Make certain that they are perfectly aligned at one end. Measure 7 or 8 inches from the aligned end and drill a hole—slightly larger than the diameter of the dowel rod—through both pieces of wood at the same time. These pieces of wood will be the supports for the swinging arm of your trebuchet. While the supports don't have to be exactly the same height, the holes you drill in them must be or the dowel rod won't rotate freely. Remove the masking tape. Glue and nail the supports to the opposite sides of the frame.

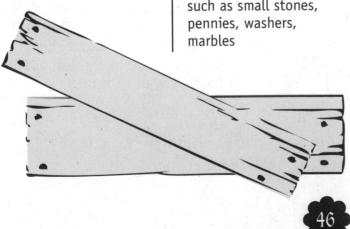

46

3 Now, make the lever arm for your trebuchet. Drill a hole slightly bigger than the diameter of the dowel halfway down the 8-inch-long piece of wood. Drill a ¼-inch hole about an inch from one end of this piece of wood. The hole at the end of the lever arm is for your weight basket.

4 Tape or glue the tuna can to the end of the lever arm without the hole, making sure that it will clear both ends of the trebuchet.

5 Make the weight basket by cutting the milk carton in half. Discard the top. Poke a hole in two opposite sides, and thread the bag tie through one of them. Thread the bag tie through the hole at the end of the lever arm and then through the other hole in the milk carton. Twist the bag tie around itself so the weight basket hangs securely on the lever arm.

6 Slide the dowel through one of the frame supports, slide the lever arm onto the dowel, and then slide the dowel into the hole in the second frame support.

7 Fill the weight basket with small stones, metal washers, or anything to give it some weight.

8 Load the tin can with your projectiles—marbles or small stones work great. Pull the tin end of the lever arm down, then let go—the weight in the weight basket will swing down and launch the projectiles from the tin. Make sure you face your trebuchet away from windows or people! Experiment with different weights and projectiles to see what works best.

Make Your Own
Marshmallow Cannon

In the Middle Ages, people created all kinds of weapons to hurl objects through the air. Here is a fun cannon you can use to hurl marshmallow cannon balls.

Supplies

sandpaper	one ½-inch PVC end cap
one 3-inch length of ½-inch PVC pipe	two ½-inch PVC elbows
three 4-inch lengths of ½-inch PVC pipe	miniature marshmallows
one ½-inch PVC tee	*Note: PVC pipe and fittings are available at any hardware store*
one 12-inch length of ½-inch PVC pipe	

1 Use sandpaper to smooth the cut edges of the PVC pipe pieces, inside and out. Make the mouthpiece by pushing an elbow onto each end of the 3-inch length of PVC, making sure that they face in opposite directions. Push a 4-inch length of PVC into one open elbow.

2 Make the cannon by pushing the tee onto one end of the 12-inch length of PVC and add a 4-inch length of PVC to both of the remaining openings. Cap the 4-inch length of PVC that is perpendicular to the 12-inch length. This will become the handle.

3 Join the cannon to the mouthpiece by pushing the only remaining open elbow onto the 4-inch length of PVC that remains open on the cannon. Make sure that the open end of the mouthpiece is the highest point on your assembled cannon.

4 To fire the cannon, place a miniature marshmallow in the opening of the mouthpiece and use a hard, puffing breath to blow it out the cannon end.

5 Use common sense when shooting your cannon. Don't point the firing end at anyone!

Castles

Today, castles seem like something out of a fairy tale, full of elegant kings and queens, knights in shining armor, feasts, and tournaments. But in reality, castle life wasn't always so grand and glamorous.

In fact, the main purpose of a castle was simply to provide safety. Castles that provided the best protection were often built upon a hill. This meant that castle dwellers had a clear view of the countryside and could see anyone approaching. Also, attacking soldiers who had to climb a hill before launching an attack were much slower than those attacking on level ground.

A castle was not just a single structure—it was more like a walled-in town. Inside, there were many separate buildings and people had all they needed for everyday life, plus the essentials of warfare. There was a stable with horses, and a **smithy**, or blacksmith, who made horseshoes, armor, and weapons. Nearly every food item necessary was grown locally. Hay, grain, and cattle were all raised outside on the estate.

The castle **keep** was the primary living area of the castle. Here there was a kitchen, and a large living and dining area sometimes known as the **Great Hall**. The Great Hall is where the nobles held court, managed business, entertained, and ate. There was little privacy in the keep. Many different people—nobles and servants alike—lived together under one roof. People not only ate in the Great Hall, but also slept there! While the court nobles may have had private **bedchambers**, the servants and less important guests did not.

Men and women slept separately. The lady of the house shared her bedchamber (and often her bed) with her ladies-in-waiting. It would be considered improper for a gentleman to enter a lady's bedchamber except in emergencies. A fancy castle might have a sitting area outside the bedchamber where noble ladies could gather to talk, sew, embroider, or sing.

DID YOU KNOW?
We don't know much about what people wore to bed, but some historians believe that kings and queens slept in the nude.

The master's private chamber was often separated from the rest of the castle only by a curtain (which isn't very private!). In a larger keep, the chamber might offer more privacy. If the noble was wealthy, it could even be very luxurious.

Walls were often painted with murals, lined with wood paneling, or plastered and whitewashed. **Tapestries** became popular

Words To Know

smithy: a blacksmith.

keep: the primary living area of the castle.

Great Hall: a large living and dining area where the nobles held court, managed business, entertained, and ate.

bedchamber: the sleeping area.

tapestries: colorful, hanging rugs that often portrayed a scene from daily life or mythology.

rushlights: lamps made of rushes, or cattails.

truckle bed: a small bed that slid under a larger bed.

for wealthy barons by the fourth century. These colorful, hanging rugs usually portrayed a scene from daily life or mythology. Tapestries were not only beautiful, but the heavy fabric over the cold stone walls also helped keep the chamber warm.

There was not much furniture inside the bedchamber—maybe a bed, a bench or stool, a candlestick, and a wooden chest. Linen drapes around the bed kept out the evening air, which people thought to be unhealthy. During the daytime hours, servants opened these draperies and the bed served as an extra seat.

When the chamber was dark, wealthy nobles used expensive beeswax candles to light the chamber. Less luxurious lighting was tallow candles, made from animal fat, **rushlights**, made of bulrushes—or cattails—dipped in tallow, or a cresset lamp, which was a metal container full of oil and a cotton wick. Except for the beeswax candles, all of these lighting options gave off lots of smoke and smelled terrible.

The master of the castle slept in the comfort of a bed, with a mattress stuffed with feathers. His attendant might share the lord's chamber and sleep in a **truckle bed** that slid under the larger bed. But the rest of the household just slept on straw mats, on benches, or on the floor of the Great Hall.

THE BAYEUX TAPESTRY

The Bayeux Tapestry is not a real tapestry, but a 70-yard long embroidered piece of linen that explains what happened before and during the famous Norman invasion of England in 1066. You simply start at the beginning and follow the story. It has even been called the first comic strip!

With all of the activity going on in the main hall, there was certainly a need for a bathroom. Most castles had small spaces called **garderobes** built into the stone walls. Inside each space was simply a raised stone platform with a hole in it. This was the bathroom. The waste dropped through the hole into a **cesspit** or the castle's moat—yet another reason to avoid swimming in the moat! There was no such thing as toilet paper in the medieval era. Instead, people used **torche-culs**— handfuls of straw or hay—or a specially made curved stick called a **gomphus**.

Even though servants washed out the garderobes frequently with buckets of water, the smell was probably awful in the main hall.

A Castle Under Siege

Castles were protected from attack by a military **garrison**, a group of soldiers. Large castles needed to be ready for military action at any time.

A castle under siege was essentially a community under lock down. The residents couldn't leave, because the attacking army would capture or kill them. The only thing the residents could do was **ration** the food and water so that it would last longer, and try to protect the castle from takeover. Every castle had a well to make sure that water was available to residents during a seige.

It was expensive to house an entire garrison, so during peacetime, the garrison was kept small. A large castle might have a garrison of one hundred military men including knights, soldiers to act as watchmen, and crossbowmen. Each member of the garrison received a daily wage as well as generous food rations.

In times of war, the garrison mobilized and recruited men from the countryside. Peasants that lived on the king or baron's land were called to duty.

The garrison fired their weapons from the castle walls or from the safety of the **arrow loop**, which was a narrow slit in the curtain wall that soldiers fired arrows through. To make these weapons even more damaging, the garrison used **Greek fire** to make flaming arrows. Greek fire was a combination of materials that was highly flammable and would stick to anything it hit, causing fires to light below. If their arrows were aimed well, the Greek fire could cause the wooden siege weapons to go up in flames. The garrison also sent Greek fire onto attackers by blowing it through tubes.

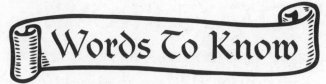

Words To Know

garderobe: the bathroom in a castle.

cesspit: a deep hole in the ground for collecting waste.

torche-culs: handfuls of straw or hay used for cleaning oneself in the bathroom.

gomphus: a curved stick used for cleaning oneself in the bathroom.

garrison: a group of soldiers ready to protect an area.

ration: limiting the amount of food and water used each day.

arrow loop: a narrow vertical slit in the curtain wall that soldiers fired arrows through.

Greek fire: a flammable material used in medieval warfare.

DID YOU KNOW?

People often kept a candle burning all night long in the bedchamber, despite the smoke and smell, to keep away pixies. These mythical creatures supposedly played mean tricks and stole things.

DID YOU KNOW?

Early castle keeps were square or rectangular. This was the quickest and easiest kind of keep to build. The problem with a four-cornered keep is that it could easily be damaged at the corners by tunneling or bombardment. By about 1150, round keeps came into fashion. The round face of a circular keep deflected arrows and even cannon fire as projectiles glanced off the face of the keep. The stability of round keeps also made it more difficult for attacking armies to undermine them by tunneling.

If attackers began climbing the castle walls, the garrison responded with a variety of tactics to knock the attackers or they dropped large rocks onto the attacking men. They poured boiling water and oil onto them. They threw sand into the faces of the approaching men. If they ran out of these things, they used anything they had available. They'd throw furniture, helmets, and even animals in an attempt to knock the attackers to the ground.

Often, it wasn't the battles that defeated a castle, but rather a lack of food. During the medieval era, it was difficult to store perishable

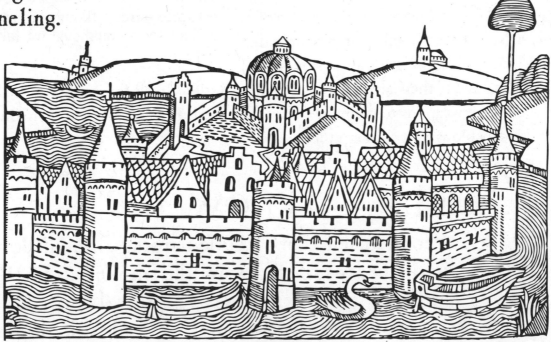

WILLIAM TELL

William Tell is the famous guy who shot an arrow through an apple that was sitting on his son's head. Could this possibly be true? Historians are still debating that! We do know that William Tell was a real person. Beyond that, no one knows for sure.

As the story goes, William neglected to bow in honor of the new leader of his town, Hermann Gessler. For this, William was arrested. His punishment was to shoot an apple off the top of his son's head, or else both would be executed. William's arrow split the apple without injuring his son, and he should have gone free. But, when Gessler asked why he brought two arrows, William told him that if he had hurt his son during this test, the second arrow would have been fired at Gessler. This angered Gessler, and William Tell was taken prisoner, though he eventually managed to escape.

foods for a long period. Too much food on hand would be wasted, but not enough in storage meant that a castle couldn't survive a siege. Castle residents had to surrender to the attacking army if they ran out of food.

Dungeons and Torture

Castles may have been home to royalty and nobles, but they also served as a place to imprison people. Dungeons were medieval prisons used to hold criminals. Sometimes people that the king or queen wanted to silence were kept there. Often, one of the castles towers served as a prison where a narrow staircase and a few guards made escape difficult. Here, prisoners lived in cold, damp, and dark conditions. Windows were rare and prisoners often sat in the dark, even during daylight hours.

Underground dungeons usually meant even harsher conditions. One kind of underground dungeon was called an **oubliette**. A trap door in the guard's room opened into a room below. Prisoners were lowered into the room by a rope. From inside this dungeon, the trap door was high in the ceiling, so escape was nearly impossible.

Words To Know

oubliette: an underground dungeon.

caltrops: sharp, pointed iron objects that that could lame a horse.

Occasionally water seeped into the dungeon. If the water became too deep, a prisoner could drown.

Even so, being sent to the dungeon was pleasant compared to the other possibility: torture. Torture was used as a punishment for some criminals. In other cases, prisoners had information and were tortured until they finally gave up and told the guards what they knew. In the most severe cases, torture was a prisoner's death sentence. It wasn't enough to simply sentence someone to death—in many cases, that death was meant to be brutally painful.

TOWER OF LONDON

One of the most famous medieval prisons is the Tower of London, which still stands today. This huge stone fortress actually has many towers. William the Conqueror built the original structure and numerous monarchs added to it in the years that followed. The Tower of London housed its first prisoner in 1100, and throughout history held many important figures, including kings, queens, and bishops.

The torture methods used in the Middle Ages were incredibly cruel. Torturers used special tools for inflicting pain. One such tool was called a thumbscrew. This was a small device that fit over a prisoner's hand. As he was questioned, a guard tightened screws that clamped the device tighter, slowly crushing the prisoner's hand.

Other torture devices were more elaborate, and likely more painful. Prisoners might be strapped into special chairs covered with metal spikes like sharp nails on the seat, back, and armrests. If that wasn't painful enough to get the victim to talk, guards heated the spikes, causing unbearable pain. Another torture device that appeared in the late Middle Ages was the rack, which slowly stretched prisoners whose hands and feet were secured to it. This stretching caused the painful dislocation of joints and even stretched muscles so severely that survivors were permanently injured. Of course, if a torture victim was subjected to the rack for too long, his limbs could actually come off.

While some medieval torture took place in torture chambers, other punishments were a public affair. Metal masks or cages that fit snugly over a naked body were perfect for public humiliation. Left caged outside, a person would suffer from the elements, facing either freezing temperatures or sunburn. These public displays of torture not only humiliated the criminal, but served as a reminder to the rest of the community that thievery, spying, or heresy would not be tolerated.

Public executions also acted as a reminder to the community about laws and proper behavior. Nobles who committed high treason—disloyalty to one's country—were beheaded. The severing of one's head from his body was considered to be an honorable way to die. These men and women faced the executioner who used a double-bladed axe or a sword to decapitate the offender. A good executioner could complete this task with one blow. To assure that the executioner did a good job, the prisoner might offer him a gold coin. A single blow was presumably less painful than multiple blows.

Heretics, people who spoke out against the church, were also executed. In 1184 the Roman Catholic Church proclaimed that burning at the stake was the official punishment for heresy.

DID YOU KNOW?

Small, four-pronged iron objects called **caltrops** were often scattered in front of castles. Caltrops always landed with one spike pointing up. These spikes could lame a horse that approached, or severely injure a man who fell upon it during a siege.

Make Your Own
Tapestry

Supplies

an old placemat in a solid, colored fabric (or a floor cloth from a craft store)

pencil

acrylic paints

paint brush

needle

embroidery thread or yarn in various colors

wooden dowel

glue

1 Sketch out a scene on the placemat. You can design it to show some aspect of medieval life or show some of the things that have happened to you recently.

2 Once you are happy with your design, paint your scene using the acrylic paints.

3 When your paint has dried, use the needle and thread to stitch outlines of some of the more important characters in your scene.

4 Glue your tapestry to the wooden dowel. Braid three long lengths of embroidery thread to make a cord, leaving several inches at each end unbraided for fringe. Tie each end to opposite ends of the wooden dowel so their fringe hangs loose. Now hang up your tapestry!

A Medieval Feast

During the spring and summer, food was plentiful. Hunting and fishing provided birds, fish, and meat. Fruits and vegetables were also available from the garden. People usually cooked apples and pears before eating them—roasted apples were popular. The wealthy began importing citrus fruits such as fresh and pickled lemons and oranges from the Mediterranean region around 1290.

Wintertime was a different story. Food could be scarce. Wild animals were difficult to find and plants did not bear fruit. To survive, people stored food in the summer so they had something to eat in the winter. Besides stored food, many castles raised pigeons and kept a fully stocked fishpond so people could eat fresh fish and poultry year-round.

MEDIEVAL MANNERS

Let worthier men help themselves before you eat, don't clutch at the best bit. Keep your hands from dirtying the cloth, and don't wipe your nose on it, or dip too deep in your cup.

When you come before a lord take off your hat or hood and fall on your right knee twice. Keep your cap off till you're told to put it on; hold up your chin; look in the lord's face; keep hand and foot still; don't spit or snot; break wind quietly; behave well.

~From *Vrbanitatis*, A Handbook of Manners (c. 1460)

In the castle kitchen, servants cooked meals over an open flame. Because of this, fire was a real and constant danger, so nobles and monarchs often built their kitchens in a separate building detached from the main hall. If a fire broke out in the kitchen, at least the main building was safe.

Nobles usually ate three times a day, but the main meal of the day was dinner, which was served at midday. A lord's dinner typically had three courses, mainly meats and pastries; bread, wine, or ale; and fruits, cheeses, and nuts. But a feast was much more elaborate.

A feast was a grand event. Feasts celebrated special events or honored guests visiting the castle. The food in itself was entertainment and often the castle cooks presented elaborately decorated platters of food. For instance, the cook might serve a whole roasted peacock that had its grand tail feathers put back in place, making for quite an impressive dish.

Words To Know

trencher: a piece of stale bread used as a plate.

mead: wine made from fermented honey.

potage: a type of vegetable soup.

pokerounce: toast spread with honey and pine nuts.

You might think the best dishes and silverware would be used at a feast, but during the Middle Ages people didn't use the same kinds of tableware that we do today. Instead of plates, diners each used a **trencher**. This was a piece of stale bread! People chose food from a common platter using their fingers, and placed their morsels on

their trencher. The only utensil that people used at a meal was a knife. This was important for cutting meat. Everyone used their fingers for all other eating. It was not acceptable to lick fingers while sharing a plate with others—talk about bad manners! Between courses, servants brought bowls of water so that everyone could clean their hands.

ON THE MENU

What does it take to feed 6,000 people? There actually was a feast with this many people in 1467, to celebrate the installation of Archbishop Neville of York. The menu included cold baked tarts, custards, spices sugared delicacies, and wafers, as well as:

- ✠ 300 quarters of wheat
- ✠ 300 casks of ale
- ✠ 100 casks of wine
- ✠ 104 oxen
- ✠ 6 wild bulls
- ✠ 1,000 sheep
- ✠ 304 calves

- ✠ 304 "porkes"
- ✠ 400 swans
- ✠ 2,000 geese
- ✠ 1,000 capons
- ✠ 2,000 pigs
- ✠ 104 peacocks

- ✠ over 13,500 other birds
- ✠ 500 stags, bucks, and roes
- ✠ 1,500 venison pies
- ✠ 608 pikes and breams
- ✠ 12 porpoises and seals
- ✠ 13,000 dishes of jelly

Make Your Own Trencher

Supplies

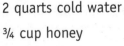

round loaf of French bread

sharp knife

1 Preheat the oven to 250 degrees Fahrenheit. Ask an adult to help you slice the bread horizontally into ½-inch-thick rounds.

2 Place the bread pieces directly onto the wire racks in your oven. Bake for about half an hour. If the bread is crispy, like toast, it's done. If not, continue baking, making sure to check it every ten minutes.

3 When the bread is done, use these trenchers instead of plates at your medieval feast. You may want to use a tablecloth!

Make Your Own Mock Mead

Mead was a sweet, alcoholic drink, but you can make a tasty version without the alcohol.

Supplies

2 quarts cold water

¾ cup honey

pitcher

1 orange

knife

cutting board

nutmeg

1 Mix the water and honey in a pitcher. Wash the orange, slice it thinly, and drop the slices into the pitcher.

2 Sprinkle with nutmeg and chill. Serve in metal or crockery mugs, if you have them.

Make Your Own Potage

Supplies

2 tablespoons olive oil

½ cup chopped onion

½ cup chopped celery

8 cups beef, chicken, or vegetable broth

2 cloves garlic, crushed

1 large potato, peeled and chopped

1 carrot, peeled and chopped

½ cup green beans

½ cup barley

½ teaspoon thyme

½ teaspoon salt

¼ teaspoon pepper

Leave out the potato if you want to make a more authentic potage. Like corn, the potato came to Europe after the Middle Ages, from the Americas.

1 Put the olive oil, onions, and celery in a Dutch oven or large pot and cook over medium heat for about 5 minutes. Stir this mixture occasionally to prevent it from burning. The celery and onions will start to look transparent.

2 Carefully pour the broth into the pot. Add all of the other ingredients. Cover the pot and bring the potage to a boil. Turn the heat to medium low and simmer for about an hour, stirring occasionally. Serve in a bowl—this is one meal that won't work with a trencher!

Make Your Own
Pokerounce

Note: Pokerounce is made of toasted bread spread with honey, spices, and nuts. You might find that this medieval treat deserves a place on modern-day menus.

Supplies

½ cup honey	6 bread slices
pinch of ground ginger	knife
pinch of cinnamon	plate
pinch of pepper	pine nuts
pinch of nutmeg	

1 Pour the honey and the spices together in a saucepan. Stir over low heat for about 5 minutes, making sure that you don't burn the honey. Remove the saucepan from the heat.

2 Toast the bread lightly and cut into quarters on the diagonal. Set them on a plate, drizzle the honey over the toast and stick the pine nuts upright into the bread. If you'd like, you can make pretty patterns with the nuts.

Villages *and the* Home

Things were quite different outside the castle walls. Small villages were scattered throughout the countryside. Life in a medieval village didn't offer much in the way of leisure or elegance. For a villager, survival meant hard work.

Farmers and tradesmen toiled to keep their families fed. Women and children worked hard to manage the household and garden. There was typically a church in every village, along with a few shops, such as a mill and a blacksmith.

Most villagers didn't own the land, but were allowed to live and farm there in exchange for providing service to the baron. These villagers were called peasants or **tenants**. Barons owned large areas of land, called manors. Barons required tenants to work a certain number of days in his service—sometimes every other day—or share a portion of their crops with him. Tenants also had to protect the baron and his lands in case of battles.

Peasants and serfs lived in simple homes. Walls were often made of clay or slabs of turf (or sod) cut from the ground. Glass was too expensive for most peasants, so windows were simply small openings. They were kept small to avoid a loss of heat.

Another method of construction used by medieval peasants was **wattle and daub**. With this method, peasants wove thin branches or vines (the wattle) between upright posts cut from logs. Then the peasants spread the daub—a mixture of clay, dung, and straw— over the wattle frame. When this was dry, they coated the walls with a lime wash that helped to make the outside water resistant and the inside brighter. Larger peasant homes might include a **byre**, or barn.

THE VILLAGE MILLER

Tenants were often forced to take their grain to the baron's mill and pay to have it ground. This was the only way they could make their daily bread. Without this requirement, villagers might grind their own grain to save money, putting the **miller** out of business. The rule meant that the miller made a good living, giving the baron a secure and well-paying tenant.

It was crucial for the roof of the house to be waterproof, but it also needed to be light enough that it didn't cause the simple structure to collapse. Peasants used reeds, straw, and heather to make a **thatched roof**. Believe it or not, these roofs could last as long as seventy years!

The Comforts of Home

The inside of a typical peasant home was very simple. In the middle of the room was the **hearth**, which provided heat and light. This was where the lady of the house did her cooking. There were no chimneys, only a hole in the roof, so homes were quite smoky.

Bedding consisted of straw tossed on the ground to form a **pallet**, or a cushioned mound. Sometime peasants stuffed straw into a sack of sorts to create a kind of mattress. They usually put this on the floor, but some peasants may have been lucky enough to have a wooden **bedstead**. Because the straw harbored pests such as lice and fleas, the peasants added insect repelling herbs to it. Even so, bug bites and itching plagued the peasants.

DID YOU KNOW?

You can grind your own grain! Ask your parents to buy some whole grains from the health food store so that you can try grinding your own. Find a smooth, flat rock for grinding on, and another that fits nicely in your hand. Thoroughly wash the rocks, pour a bit of grain onto the flat rock and crush the grains with the hand-held rock into a fine flour.

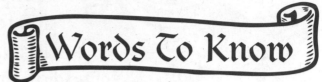

Words To Know

tenant: someone who pays rent to use land or buildings owned by someone else.

miller: a man who ground grain into flour for bread.

wattle and daub: a building method using small branches and vines (the wattle) and a mixture of clay, dung, and straw (the daub) to hold the branches together.

byre: a barn.

thatched roof: a roof made of dried plant materials such as reeds, straw, and heather.

hearth: an open fireplace in the center of a house.

pallet: a sleeping surface that was a kind of cushioned mound.

bedstead: a bed frame.

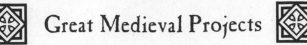

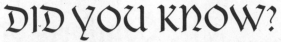

DID YOU KNOW?

People cleared much of the countryside for agricultural purposes, so wood was a valuable resource in most villages. Instead of cutting down an entire tree for firewood, peasants used a practice called **coppicing**, which left the trunk of a tree intact to keep growing, but required that the uppermost branches be cut. Since these thin sticks didn't burn as well as big logs, peasants bound them together into tight bundles.

The kitchen was just as spare as the rest of the house. Cooking and eating utensils were usually made of clay or wood. A knife was an important part of everyone's belongings. People speared morsels of food with the tip of the blade and ate the food right off the knife.

There was no running water in these simple homes, nor throughout most of Europe. Peasant women fetched water from a well or nearby stream and hauled it to their homes. They probably kept a cauldron of water over the fire at all times, in order to have hot water when needed.

Peasants usually ate only two meals each day. Breakfast as we know it didn't exist, though a peasant might grab a piece of bread and dip it into his mug of ale or wine in the morning. Peasants ate their first and biggest meal of the day, called dinner, at midday. This meal probably consisted of some sort of stew or porridge, bread, and vegetables. In the evening, a lighter meal called supper often included soup.

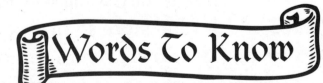

Words To Know

coppicing: a method for harvesting wood that allowed the tree to continue growing.

famine: a shortage of food.

MEDIEVAL HYGIENE

Peasants bathed in streams when it was warm. They didn't bathe much in the winter because carrying water and heating it over the fire was a lot of work. Nobles had servants to do the hard work, so they bathed more often. The hot water for nobles was sometimes perfumed with rose petals. Some castles had a room next to the kitchen that served as a bathing room. Ladies gathered here to bathe in parties.

Even if people didn't bathe their entire bodies, they did wash parts of their bodies regularly. Because people ate food with their fingers, it was common courtesy to wash their hands frequently at mealtimes.

Shaving was uncommon, because it was difficult and painful to get a clean shave with a razor that resembled a carving knife. Haircutting, too, was a chore. Scissors were available, but they were the squeeze type, similar to old-fashioned grass shears.

There is evidence that some people cared for their teeth during the Middle Ages. Toothbrushes were unheard of until the thirteenth century. Even then, only nobles had them. But people did use green twigs and wool cloth to scrub their teeth clean.

The food on a medieval table came directly from the surrounding area, either from crops or from the wild. If a crop failed, it could easily lead to **famine**. There were no grocery stores and certainly no extra money to spend even if there had been!

Many peasants kept a cow and some chickens. Since fresh milk was hard to store, peasants churned most of it into butter or made it into cheese. As an alternative to animal milk, people made something called almond milk. It wasn't really milk, but rather a combination of ground almonds and water cooked to a milky consistency.

Meat was a luxury. When farmers butchered a large animal, it was more meat than a single family could eat before it went bad. To keep meat for longer periods, people packed it in salt. The salt removed the moisture from the meat, preventing decay. Salt was a valuable resource.

DID YOU KNOW?

Some peasant homes offered shelter not only to a family, but also to the family's animals. The animals were fenced off from the area in which the family lived, but surely there was still quite a stink!

Vegetables kept for several months if they were stored in a cold cellar. Peasants also dried grapes to make raisins. Grain was very important, and was used to make porridge and bread. If a peasant's grain stores were ruined by moisture or rodents, it could mean a winter of hunger.

Women and Families

The Medieval church taught women to obey the men in their lives. Women were considered inferior to men. But medieval women had a lot of responsibility and were hardly inferior, especially when it came to work.

A common medieval woman had many household duties. She was responsible for housework, cooking, raising children, and making clothing. She might also raise chickens and grow a garden. During harvest season, peasant women helped in the fields, right alongside the men. Some even earned extra money by hiring themselves out to neighboring farms.

PARISHES

The countryside was divided into areas called **parishes**. A parish could be one village or several villages. Each parish had its own church. The church was plain and simple, but certainly a more impressive building than most of the village homes. The inside of many parish churches boasted brightly colored murals featuring biblical stories.

The church was a big part of village life. The parish priest offered Mass for his parishioners each Sunday and also celebrated holy days. It's unlikely that everyone from the village made it to Mass each Sunday, but on days of major feasts, such as Christmas and Easter, the church was probably full.

Every villager had to pay money to the church, called a **tithe**. Tithes were a portion of each household's animals and crops. This money kept the church in good condition, paid the priest a good salary, and helped the poor.

OUTBUILDINGS

For a toilet, the peasants used a **privy**, which was a small structure separate from the house. Underneath the privy was a cesspit—a deep hole in the ground—to catch waste. At night, or in bad weather, people used chamber pots inside the home, which they later emptied into the cesspit. When the cesspit became full, peasants dumped the waste in the fields as fertilizer. Other outbuildings included a "cow house" for cows, a stable for horses, a pigsty, a henhouse, and a barn.

Behind the cottage was the peasant's plot of land or **croft**. It was generally around half an acre in size. Here, the peasant and his wife might grow grain, vegetables, or fruit. This is also where his animals grazed.

Fathers sometimes passed on their skills to their daughters, usually when a man had no sons. These trained women worked as bakers, spinners, alewives (women who brewed ale), and weavers. In spite of all this, women received little respect from men.

Interestingly, unmarried women had the same rights as men. However, upon marrying, a common woman gave up her land and her rights to her husband.

Life for a noble woman was quite different. A wealthy lady did not have to worry about

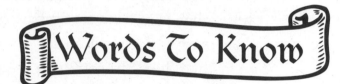

Words To Know

parishes: a division of land that had its own church.

tithe: a portion of each household's animals and crops paid to the church.

privy: a small toilet structure, separate from the house.

croft: a peasant's plot of land, usually used for farming.

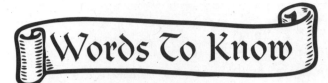

Words To Know

brocade: fabric woven with elaborate designs.

midwife: a woman who is skilled in helping birth babies.

earning a living. Instead, she focused on fulfilling the proper social roles required of her position. A noble woman needed to always behave properly in order to maintain her social status and spent a good amount of time worrying about how she was dressed. She was in charge of running the household, making sure that it ran smoothly. She made certain that the larder was full, organized the staff, and even arranged for the defense of the castle when her husband was away.

Marriage was not very romantic during the Middle Ages. For the noble class, it was a chance to form an alliance with another important family. Because many nobles married for position rather than love, it could be a lonely life for a newly married woman, especially if she left her homeland and friends behind in order to fulfill her obligation.

CLOTHING

Medieval peasants dressed in homemade woolen clothes and wore hoods. Nobles had a much broader choice of what to wear. While woolen clothes were also a part of their wardrobe, they could afford to import expensive cloth, such as silk, velvet, or **brocade**.

Special laws called sumptuary laws actually told people how to dress. Each social class was required to dress within certain guidelines. This made it easy to tell a person's social status simply by looking at his clothing. Even if a peasant could afford a fancy piece of clothing, he couldn't wear it because he was not of the proper class.

Peasants used natural dyes to color the fabric that would become their clothing. Most of the colors were pretty dull, though some more vibrant colors were made. Brighter colors were harder to achieve and highly prized (and priced!) so often only wealthy people wore them.

A BABY'S CHRISTENING

At the wedding ceremony, the bride and groom brought witnesses who could attest to the event. To help them remember, witnesses often hit each other! Following the ceremony, friends showered the bride and groom with seeds, shouting "Plenty! Plenty!" The seeds symbolized fertility and the wish that a couple would have many children. This custom remains with us today in the form of wedding guests throwing rice or birdseed at a newly married couple.

A baby was christened as soon as possible after birth, so that the devil couldn't carry off its soul. One godparent held the baby's body, and two more held each one of the baby's legs. Then the priest completely submerged the baby in holy water. The godparents then promised to keep the baby from water, fire, horse's foot, and hound's tooth for seven years.

The birth of a baby was an exciting time in any household. A **midwife** helped deliver the baby. She massaged its fingers, arms, and legs to chase away evil. Then she rubbed the baby with salt and honey and sometimes laid the newborn on a bed of rose leaves. She rubbed the inside of the baby's mouth with honey, and then filled her own mouth with wine and spit a few drops into the baby's mouth. Finally, she wrapped the infant in soft cloths. A noble baby would be wrapped in silk, fur, or ermine.

DID YOU KNOW?

Young, unmarried women wore their hair loose. Married women covered their hair with a linen cloth called a wimple.

It was very common for babies to die within their first year of life. If they survived, they had a childhood much like that of children today. They played games of chase, hide and seek, and war. They had toys like dolls, wooden soldiers, and jumping jacks. Women taught children basic household skills, such as how to make a bed and set a table. When a noble boy reached his eighth birthday, he was usually sent to be a page in another castle. This was because his parents thought he would become too "soft" from the care of women.

Make Your Own Almond Milk

Supplies

1½ cups raw almonds
(or you can substitute walnuts)

2 cups water

saucepan

sieve

spoon

bowl

1 Ask an adult to help you bring the water to a boil. Grind the nuts in a coffee grinder or blender.

2 Stir the ground-up nuts into the boiling water, cover, and remove from heat. Set the mixture aside to cool, but come back to stir it occasionally.

3 Pour the cooled mixture into a fine sieve and use the spoon to push through as much liquid as you can, catching the almond milk in the bowl.

DID YOU KNOW?

During the Middle Ages people believed water to be unhealthy, which was often true. Instead they drank ale or wine—sometimes watered down—for good health. Or they drank almond milk. Since the water was boiled first, it was safe to drink.

Make Your Own
Butter

Supplies

½ pint of heavy whipping cream

1-pint glass jar with a tight-fitting lid

1 Bring the whipping cream to room temperature. Thoroughly wash and dry the glass jar. Pour the whipping cream into the jar and secure the lid tightly.

2 Shake the jar back and forth quickly. After about 10 or 15 minutes of continual shaking, you'll feel the liquid in the jar change as the fat solidifies and hits the side of the jar. Shake a few more times, then check inside the jar. You should see a ball of butter sitting in the "butter milk."

3 Pour off the liquid and add a little water to the jar. Replace the lid and shake again. Drain the butter and place it on a serving dish. Enjoy your homemade butter on a slice of fresh bread.

DID YOU KNOW?

Peasants collected the drippings from meat as it was cooking by placing a tray below the roasting spit. The peasants used these drippings to flavor their foods or to oil their boots!

Make Your Own
Insect Repellent

The fleas common in bedding during the Middle Ages plagued peasants and royalty alike. Dried herbs mixed into the straw tick eased the trouble somewhat, but herbalists mixed herbs with water or honey to make medieval insect repellants.

Supplies

small glass container, such as a baby-food jar

20 drops eucalyptus essential oil

20 drops rosemary essential oil

10 drops citronella essential oil

2 ounces olive oil

1 Mix all of the ingredients together in the glass container.

2 Rub some of the scented oil on exposed skin before you head outside. Be careful to avoid the area right around your eyes.

3 You can also put several drops of the oil on a small square of scrap fabric to place inside your pillow-case to repel bugs. Of course, your bed is probably much less buggy than a peasant's bed was!

DID YOU KNOW?

"Sleep tight, don't let the bed bugs bite," is an expression that we still use. It comes from Medieval times when bed bugs were a common problem.

Make Your Own
Thatched Roof

Supplies

scissors

half-gallon milk container

6 craft sticks

glue

dried plant materials from your yard

string

watering can

1 Cut the milk jug as shown. Cut equally spaced slits into the angled side of the milk carton and push the craft sticks into the slits. Glue for extra stability.

3 Tie the bundles of dried materials onto the bottom craft stick on each side, with the untied ends hanging toward the ground. When these craft sticks are full, move up to the next craft stick, allowing thatch to overlap the first layer. Continue adding bundles until both sides of the roof are completely covered. Attach more bundles along the pointed peak of the roof to cover the gap at the top.

2 Gather your dried plant materials into small bundles and tie them together at one end.

4 Test your thatched roof to see if you'd be dry during the Middle Ages. If you have a watering can, you can use that to make it "rain." If not, just use a kitchen cup and slowly drip water onto the roof. Peek in through the door to see if your thatched roof kept out the rain.

Make Your Own Hennin

In the late Middle Ages,
noble ladies wore a tall, pointy hat
called a hennin.

Supplies

sheet of poster board	clear tape
yard stick	hole punch
pencil	fabric, ribbon, and buttons
scissors	glue

1 Choose one corner of the poster board to be the point of the hennin. From this corner, measure and mark 18 inches in either direction. Connect your marks with a curved line as shown.

2 Cut along the curved line. Roll the poster board into a cone shape. Adjust the size of the opening to fit your head comfortably and tape to secure. Punch holes at each side of the opening. Tie a 12-inch length of ribbon into each hole. Use the ribbons to tie the hennin in place on your head.

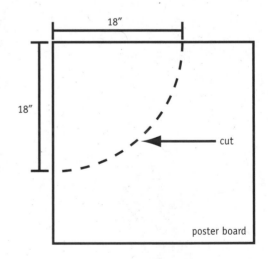

3 Decorate the cone by gluing on fabric to cover the poster board and add several long lengths of ribbon at the cone. You can use the buttons to make it fancy.

Medieval
Cities and Towns

Even during the Middle Ages there were large cities like Paris and London. These cities looked quite different than they do today!

Cities had three main areas: the church or cathedral, the marketplace, and the castle. Medieval cities were not planned the way our modern cities are. Buildings were erected and streets were made as they were needed, giving the city an unorganized feel. For defensive purposes, people erected walls around the city. Their homes were constructed very close together so that everyone could fit inside the safety of the walls. This made for crowded living.

Smaller "market towns" might have fewer than 500 residents. It wasn't the size or population of the town that made it different from a rural village, but rather the services provided. These towns had a marketplace, tradesmen's shops, and sometimes even an overnight facility for travelers. Situated in a large open area, the marketplace was where vendors hawked their wares.

All kinds of people lived in a city. There were wealthy merchants, bakers, butchers, glassblowers, servants, and street cleaners. In spite of the different lives they led, these city dwellers had one thing in common: they didn't want a ruler. They wanted to govern themselves. These independent cities were called **communes**.

Medieval cities were densely populated. Just imagine the noise as residents mingled with carts, horses, and other animals in the crowded narrow streets! The streets were made of packed mud or sometimes **cobbled.** Cobbled streets were paved with fist-sized round stones. Mud streets were fine during dry weather, but when it rained they were messy. The streets were also dark and narrow because the upper stories of the buildings stuck out over the streets, blocking out the sunlight.

DID YOU KNOW?
Medieval cities were small by today's standards. Paris was one of the larger medieval cities and was home to less than 200,000 people. Today, Paris is home to more than 2 million people.

Not only were cities crowded, but they were quite dirty. People disposed of household and human waste in pits behind their homes. There wasn't proper drainage, so when it rained the waste flowed through the streets and eventually got into the drinking water supply.

HOMES IN THE CITY

In the early Middle Ages, city homes were simple, single story cottages. As the population grew, houses got taller. The lower floors were typically reserved for shops and businesses. Since a working shop was not the best place to sell items, the shopkeeper displayed his wares on a table in front of his shop.

Glass was expensive and used only for churches or royal palaces. Wealthy city dwellers made their windowpanes from the horns of cows and sheep. The horn was not see-through like glass, but it did allow light into a home without allowing precious heat to escape.

Fire was a big danger in these closely-built cities. If a building caught on fire, it could easily spread, causing major damage to the city. Each evening a **curfew** bell rang to remind residents to put out all fires and lights and go to bed. This curfew also helped to eliminate troublesome activity that might happen at night if residents wandered about freely.

Other health hazards came in the form of rats, mice, flies, fleas, and lice. The garbage and dung in the yards and streets provided the perfect conditions for them, and they brought something of their own to medieval Europe: the **plague**.

The Plague

The plague—sometimes called the Black Death—struck medieval Europe in the middle of the fourteenth century. Rats and mice carried **bubonic plague**. When fleas bit these rodents, they took in infected blood. If the infected flea jumped onto a person and bit him, a small amount of the infected blood passed into the person's bloodstream. Of course, during the Middle Ages, people didn't know this.

The bubonic plague started with flu-like symptoms. Soon lumps that could be as large as oranges appeared all over the body, turned black,

Words To Know

communes: cities that governed themselves.

cobbles: fist-sized round stones used to pave roads.

curfew: a certain time by which people are required to be in their homes.

plague: an infectious disease.

bubonic plague: an infectious disease carried by rats and mice that spread to humans.

(hence the nickname Black Death,) and oozed blood and pus. While it was possible to recover from the plague, and some did, it was unlikely.

The devastation from this disease was immense. Without modern-day medicine, or knowledge of how to prevent the spread of the disease, the plague passed quickly from person to person. About half of the people in Europe died between 1347 and 1351. Plague-infested cities were often completely abandoned.

As the plague spread, people accused others of poisoning the water or the air, causing this mysterious disease. Mobs of angry people searching for someone to blame rounded up suspects and burned or drowned them.

Another common disease in the Middle Ages was **leprosy**. This severe skin disease caused sores and numbness. It could eventually lead to disfiguration and the loss of fingers and toes. People infected with this disease were called **lepers**.

Because the disease was highly contagious, people avoided lepers at all costs. Many lepers were sent away to special colonies where they stayed until they died. When lepers walked down the street, they carried a bell or clapper that warned people to get away.

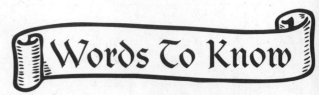

Words To Know

leprosy: a severe skin disease.
leper: person infected with leprosy.
humor: an element of the body: blood, yellow bile, phlegm, and black bile.
apothecary: a medieval pharmacist.
opiates: drugs used as pain relievers.
guild: an organization established to protect merchants.

HERBAL REMEDIES

During the Middle Ages, only the wealthiest people could afford to be treated by a doctor. Many women learned traditional herbal skills as part of their household training. Poorer people depended upon these local folk medicine practitioners.

Medieval Medicine

During the Middle Ages, doctors believed that the body had four **humors**: blood, yellow bile, phlegm, and black bile. Doctors thought that in order to be healthy, the body's humors had to be in balance. To create this balance, doctors used a treatment called bloodletting. A doctor would cut open a vein and allow blood to drain from the body. This method was rarely successful, and patients often died because of it.

Doctors did not provide medicine to a patient. That job fell to a tradesman called an **apothecary**, who was like a pharmacist. Doctors didn't do surgery, either. This was the barber's job! Besides providing a shave and a haircut, barbers performed surgery and extracted bad teeth. Unfortunately for the patients, anesthesia was unavailable. Patients had to bite down on a piece of leather to help them stand the pain. Sometimes they breathed in vapors from **opiates** to relieve the pain.

Medieval Trades and Jobs

During the Middle Ages, virtually all work was done by hand. There was great need for people to perform a variety of tasks in order to keep a village or city functioning. Blacksmiths made tools and weapons. Chandlers made candles. A scullion washed and cleaned the kitchen. The ewerer heated water and brought it in for a noble's bath. And the gong farmer emptied cesspits full of waste with a shovel and buckets.

DID YOU KNOW?

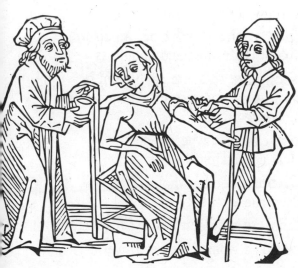

Just like doctors today, medieval doctors tested a patient's urine. But they tested it by tasting it! The sweetness or acidity of the urine helped doctors make their diagnosis. Patients would carry their urine samples to their doctor in a special flask. The urine flask was so common that it became a symbol for the medical profession.

Medieval tradesmen belonged to organizations called **guilds**. Guilds were very important for a member's social and professional life. Guilds made sure that business competition was fair. They set prices, made sure that the items sold were of good quality, and managed the training of apprentices. They also arranged feasts and celebrations for its members, and took care of a member's family if he died. Members worked through three phases to become an elite member of a medieval guild:

✠ **Apprentice:** A medieval guild apprentice trained with a master. Apprentices usually began work in their early teens. The apprenticeship lasted between five and nine years depending on the trade. During this time the apprentice received only his board (meals), lodging, and training—no wages.

MEDIEVAL JOBS

board-hewers: worked in the forest making boards and beams for building.

bottler: in charge of the buttery, where the wine and ale was stored.

butler: cared for the cellar and the butts (bottles) of wine and beer and managed the brewing staff.

cottars: lowly peasants who worked as swineherds, prison guards, and other odd jobs.

ditcher: worker who dug moats, vaults, foundations, and mines.

ewerer: a man who heated the bath water for a noble.

gong farmer: a person who emptied cesspits full of waste using only a shovel and buckets.

hayward: someone who tended the hedges and fences.

herald: a knight's assistant and an expert advisor on heraldry.

keeper of the wardrobe: a person in charge of the tailors and laundress.

messengers: servants of the lord or baron who carried receipts, letters, and commodities.

minstrels: men who provided musical entertainment.

scullion: a person who washed and cleaned the kitchen.

shearmen: a person who trimmed cloth.

spinster: a woman who spun yarn.

✠ **Journeyman:** After serving as an apprentice for many years, a man became a journeyman. A journeyman still worked for his master, but received wages for his labor. During his time as a journeyman, he created his masterpiece. He presented his masterpiece to the guild as evidence of his craftsmanship in the hope of being accepted as a master.

✠ **Master:** A master craftsman was allowed to set up his own workshop and train apprentices. The first few years of a master's business was a trial period. During this time, a master paid higher taxes to the king for the privilege of doing business.

MEDIEVAL TRADES

baker: someone who made bread and other baked goods.

blacksmith: a tradesman who worked with iron to make metal implements such as tools, weapons, and horseshoes.

butcher: a person who slaughtered animals and prepared the meat for market.

carpenter: a tradesman who constructed things from wood, such as homes and furniture.

chandler: a tradesman who made candles.

cooper: a tradesman who made and repaired barrels and tubs.

dyer: someone who dyed cloth and yarn in huge heated vats.

fuller: a worker who thickened cloth by wetting and beating the material.

glassblower: a tradesman who made glass objects.

hatmaker: a maker of hats.

jeweler: maker of jewelry.

mason: a bricklayer.

pastrycook: a baker specializing in pastries.

saddler: a maker of saddles.

shoemaker: a tradesman who made and repaired shoes.

stonecutter: someone who cut or carved stone.

tailor: a tradesman who made and repaired clothing.

tanner: a preparer of leather.

weaver: a tradesman who wove cloth and tapestries.

Markets and Fairs

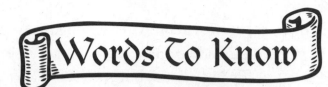

Words To Know

Shrove Tuesday: the day before the Christian season of Lent.

Lent: a season of fasting for the forty days before Easter.

Large cities had weekly markets. You could buy just about anything at these markets: cheese, eggs, salt, shoes, pots, pans, tools, and knives. People traveled as much as six or seven miles to come to market.

Because there was no refrigeration, meat spoiled quickly, making it a hard item to sell. Instead, peddlers herded animals like cows, pigs, sheep, and geese into the market area. They sold the animals while they were still alive, and the shopper walked the animal to his home for butchering.

On religious holidays such as **Shrove Tuesday**, large banquets and festivities took place. These fairs lasted for days, some as long as a week or two. Merchants traveled from fair to fair to sell their wares. Everyone looked forward to taking a break from work and having fun at the fair. Taverns and alehouses were filled with people drinking, and there was entertainment by jugglers, acrobats, and even dancing bears. There was also food for sale, such as meat pies, spiced almonds, and pretzels.

Make Your Own
Spiced Almonds

Supplies

¼ cup sugar	mixing bowl
1 teaspoon cinnamon	spoon
¼ teaspoon nutmeg	1½ cups whole raw almonds
¼ teaspoon salt	aluminum foil
1 egg white	oven
1 teaspoon water	

1 Mix sugar, spices, and salt in a mixing bowl. Whisk in the egg white and water.

2 Stir the almonds into the spice mixture, coating the nuts thoroughly.

3 Line a cookie sheet with aluminum foil and spread the almonds evenly onto it.

4 Bake the almonds at 300 degrees Fahrenheit for about 30 minutes, stirring every 5 to 10 minutes to prevent the almonds from sticking. They are ready when they are golden brown. Make sure not to burn them!

5 Once the almonds cool, you can serve them in a paper cup or a bowl.

Make Your Own
Pretzels

Supplies

For the dough:

Mixing bowls

1½ cups warm water

1⅛ teaspoon active dry yeast

spoon

2 tablespoons brown sugar

1⅛ teaspoon salt

3 cups all-purpose flour

1 cup wheat flour

cooking oil

cloth towel

oven

baking sheet

For the bath:

2 cups warm water

2 tablespoons baking soda

slotted spoon

For the topping:

4 tablespoons melted butter

coarse salt or cinnamon sugar for topping

DID YOU KNOW?

Bread was an important part of the diet during the middle ages, and bakers sometimes cheated their customers by giving them less than they paid for. When laws were passed to prevent that, those bakers started giving "a baker's dozen," meaning thirteen. In this way they avoided being harshly punished for miscounting and giving less than a dozen.

1 Pour warm water into a mixing bowl. Sprinkle yeast onto the water, then stir in sugar and salt to dissolve. Stir in flour until the dough forms a ball.

2 Knead the dough until it's smooth and elastic. You can do this in a mixer if you have one. If not, once your dough has formed a ball, turn it out onto a floured surface and use your hands to knead the dough. Push with the heel of your hand and fold the dough over, working it until it's nice and smooth. This can take several minutes.

THE ORIGIN OF THE PRETZEL

Legend has it that in the year 610, religious men called monks made scraps of dough into strips and shaped them to represent a child's arms folded in prayer. The monks called this bread a pretiola, Latin for "little reward." They gave them to children as a reward for learning their prayers. Other people liked these little treats, too. As the pretiola grew in popularity, it made its way to Austria and Germany, where people called it a bretzel, or pretzel.

Soon the twisted shape of the pretzel came to represent good luck and prosperity. At weddings, the bride and groom broke a pretzel between them the same way that we pull on a wishbone today.

Made without eggs, milk, butter, or lard, pretzels were an acceptable food during the forty-day religious season of Lent. Lent began on Ash Wednesday and lasted until the day before Easter. The church forbade people to eat meat or any animal products during this time. Medieval pretzels were not like the hard, crunchy snacks that we eat today. More likely, they were a bit chewy and perhaps coated with sugar.

3 Place the dough in a greased bowl and cover loosely with a towel. Let it rise in a warm place for half an hour.

4 While the dough is rising, prepare a water bath with 2 cups of warm water and the baking soda.

5 To make the pretzels, pinch off golf-ball-sized pieces of dough and roll them into a half-inch-thick rope, about 12 inches long. Shape into the "crossed arms" of a pretzel. If your dough is a little sticky, sprinkle a little flour on your work surface and roll the pretzel in it as you work.

6 With a slotted spoon, dip the pretzel into the baking soda solution making certain to stir the solution often as you dip the pretzel dough. Drain each pretzel and place on a greased baking sheet, leaving an inch or two between each pretzel. Let pretzels rise in a warm place for about half an hour. Meanwhile, preheat oven to 450 degrees Fahrenheit.

7 Bake for about 10 minutes or until golden. When the pretzels come out of the oven, brush them with melted butter and sprinkle them with coarse salt or cinnamon sugar.

Make Your Own
Clapper

Lepers used clappers to alert passers-by to stay away from them. You can make your own clappers and play games with them.

1 Use the hammer and nail to make a hole near the center of each plastic bottle cap.

2 Tie a knot in the middle of each rubber band. Make sure that one loop of each rubber band fits your finger snugly.

3 Push the loops of one rubber band into the hole in one of the bottle caps from the inside. You can use the toothpick to make this easier. Do the same with the second rubber band and bottle cap.

4 To use your clappers, slip one onto your thumb and the other onto your middle finger and bang them together. Can you imagine having to make noise to warn people away?

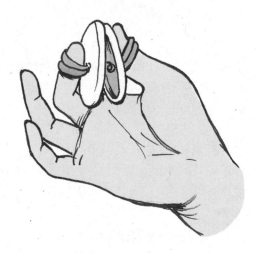

Supplies

hammer and nail	two rubber bands
two plastic bottle caps	toothpick

Medieval *Beliefs*

The Medieval Christian church was very powerful, and the majority of people were Christian. The church had its own laws, and often told kings what to do.

People who spoke out against the church were called **heretics**. If discovered, they could be brought to trial and sentenced to whipping or, even worse, to be burned at the stake.

Non-Christians, specifically Jews and Muslims, were a minority in medieval Europe. For a time, Christians and Jews lived together in relative peace. However, few Jews were able to own land or belong to guilds. This made it difficult for them to earn a living.

DID YOU KNOW?

One group of people, the Cathars of France, rejected the teachings of the Catholic Church. In 1208, the Pope ordered a **crusade** against these heretics that lasted for 26 years. During this time, crusaders slaughtered, tortured, and burned thousands of Cathars in bonfires until there were none left.

To make money, many Jews bcame moneylenders or **usurers**. Part of a usurer's job was to collect unpaid debts. This didn't make the Jews very popular, but it did make them wealthy. In 1290, King Edward I of England ordered every Jew to leave his domain. They were allowed to take their personal property, but land was turned over to the crown. The Jews weren't allowed to return until 1655.

Prior to the spread of the Christian religion, people's spiritual practices varied, according to their personal beliefs, and probably influenced somewhat by the region in which they lived. These people followed **pagan** beliefs, though paganism isn't a single religion. Paganism included any type of worship that was not Christian, Jewish, or Islamic. Pagans followed what Christians believed were false gods. They worshipped the natural world and often multiple gods.

Words To Know

heretic: someone who speaks out against the church.

usurers: moneylenders who charged interest on their loans.

pagan: a non-Christian who worshipped the natural world and many different gods.

Holy Grail: the mythical vessel said to have been used by Jesus.

The church forced many pagans to convert to Christianity. Even so, those people couldn't quite give up many of their traditional beliefs or the woodland gods that were familiar to them. Many continued some pagan practices in secret. The Catholic Church denounced these practices, but ironically, many pagan customs found their way into the church's rituals.

Even the story of the legendary **Holy Grail**—a story that is Christian in nature—apparently has roots in pagan lore, as does the tradition of bringing an evergreen tree inside to celebrate Christmas.

DID YOU KNOW?

Some medieval magicians were considered **alchemists**. These magicians worked to change metal to gold. They believed that accomplishing this would change a man's spiritual nature and purify the soul. Of course, there were probably more than a few alchemists who thought that changing metal to gold would be good for their pocketbook!

Witchcraft and Sorcery

Today, we imagine that witches wear tall, pointy black hats, have warts on their noses, and fly on broomsticks. Turning a witch into a comical character could have made the possibility of witches less scary. During medieval times, witches—or people thought to be witches—looked much like you do.

Sorcerers and witches were humans who didn't follow the rules of the church. They predicted the future by examining entrails (guts!), bones, numbers, mirrors, water, or wine. In an attempt to understand the universe, they studied herbs, plants, rocks, animals, and the stars. They cast spells and said incantations in an effort to make things happen.

Did these medieval witches really have supernatural powers? No one knows, but today some people still believe in witch-craft. Even if witches and sorceers couldn't really work magic, during the Middle Ages people were wary of them because it was thought that they worshipped the power of evil.

Witchcraft and sorcery are based in magic. During the Middle Ages people believed that magic could only be accomplished with the help of demons or a pact with the devil. As you might imagine, the church had a problem with this! In 1484 Pope Innocent the VIII wrote a document giving his blessing to the act of witch hunting.

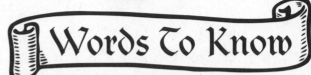

Words To Know

alchemist: someone who practices alchemy.

alchemy: a medieval chemical science that tried to change regular metal into gold, discover a universal cure for disease, and prolong life forever.

alms: giving money or food to the poor.

DID YOU KNOW?

Each day of the year is a designated feast day to honor a specific saint or holy person.

Patron Saints

Patron saints are special guardians over specific areas of life. There are patron saints for almost everything, including each trade or profession, and for every illness. Bernadine of Siena is the patron saint of advertisers. Rita of Cascia is the patron saint of parents. And Catherine of Alexandria is the patron saint of librarians. People prayed to their saints in times of need.

You may have seen statues of Saint Francis of Asissi. He's often wearing long robes, with his hands outstretched to forest animals. That's because Saint Francis is the patron saint of animals, birds, and the environment. It's common for churches to have celebrations honoring animals on his feast day, October 4th.

Francis was a charitable man. One story tells of a time that he was selling expensive cloth for his father. When a beggar approached asking for **alms**, Francis completed his business deal and then chased after the beggar and gave him everything he had. His father was not happy.

Francis found his calling with the church and founded the Order of Friars Minor, otherwise known as the Franciscans. He also founded the Order of Poor Dames for women. This group is also known as the Poor Clares and is still in operation with as many as 20,000 Poor Clare nuns in the world.

DID YOU KNOW?

Saint Francis set up the first known three-dimension nativity scene in celebration of Christmas, using real animals to create a live scene.

While praying during a forty-day fasting period, Francis had a vision and was left with special marks called stigmata. Stigmata are wounds or marks that occur in the same places where Jesus was injured during his crucifixion. Upon his death, the church viewed this vision and stigmata as sufficient reason to make him a saint.

JOAN OF ARC

Joan of Arc lived a short but eventful life in France. She was an obedient child and cared for others. When Joan was thirteen, she believed that God spoke to her. For years she heard voices. Then one day God told her to do something extraordinary. She was supposed to drive the English army out of France! Then she was to take Charles, the eldest son of the king of France, to a city called Reims for his coronation.

People couldn't believe that a teenage girl wanted to do such a dangerous thing. But Joan was persistent. She finally convinced the Archbishop of Reims to allow her to lead an army against the English. Amazingly, she won the battle and drove the English out of France. Following this success, Charles was crowned king. Joan's vision had come true!

Later, Joan was captured and turned over to the English, who wanted to kill her. She was eventually condemned as a witch and burned at the stake in 1431. At the time of her death, Joan was only 19 years old. Nearly 500 years later, the Church of Rome declared Joan to be a saint.

Pilgrims

Holy relics were items that Christian people considered **sacred**. Some holy relics were things that we would consider gross today—the bones and teeth of saints or even their skulls! People believed these relics held miraculous powers. Churches displayed their holy relics in very fancy containers called **reliquaries**. If a person lived far from a relic, he or she had to travel to go see it. This journey was called a **pilgrimage** and the people making the journey were called **pilgrims**.

DID YOU KNOW?

Some knights had holy relics embedded into the hilt of their sword. They believed this protected them from danger in battle.

Pilgrimages had a festive feel as rich and poor traveled together, often singing and playing pipes along the way. A pilgrimage was an opportunity for people to see different parts of the world after spending much of their lives in one place.

One reason that people went "on pilgrimage" rather than "on vacation" is that pilgrims were seen as a special group of people. They were free to pass through enemy countries. They sometimes traveled with armed soldiers. Even with this protection, bands of robbers sometimes attacked the pilgrims.

Pilgrimages were expensive and risky. Pilgrims could not not work during the time they were gone, and they also had to pay for food and accommodations along the way. Traveling during the Middle Ages was difficult. The roads were rough, and in many cases, there were only paths on which to walk. These roads and paths were not well marked and pilgrims easily got lost.

Pilgrimages were a very important part of medieval life. In a world without electricity, telephones, or even a post office, people relied on these travelers for news of the world.

Words To Know

holy relics: items that the Christian people considered sacred.

sacred: highly valued and important.

reliquary: a fancy container used to hold holy relics.

pilgrimage: a trip made to visit a holy relic or sacred place.

pilgrim: a person making a pilgrimage.

caravan: a large group of people traveling together.

THE SILK ROAD

Pilgrims weren't the only people in Medieval Europe who traveled long distances. Traders went halfway around the world buying and selling goods. The most important trade route in the Middle Ages was called the Silk Road. It wasn't really a road, nor was it made of silk. Rather, it was a collection of different routes over land, and even sea, between Europe and Asia. Silk was one of the items carried along this route. Merchants traveled in **caravans**, which is a large group of people traveling together. Silk wasn't the only thing traded along this route. European traders took gold, ivory, precious stones, and glass to China. They brought furs, pottery, jade, and iron back to Europe.

The Silk Road also carried information. It was a way for people to learn about faraway people, the latest ideas, and news of the world.

DID YOU KNOW?

There were guidebooks written just for pilgrims. One called **The Guide for Pilgrims to Santiago** described some of the dangers that a pilgrim faced, including thick forests, mosquito-infested marshes, wild animals, impassable rivers, and undrinkable water.

Most pilgrims traveled on foot. As you might imagine, this was a slow process. Pilgrims covered about twenty miles a day. Wealthier pilgrims might travel on horseback, which was the fastest method of travel available during the medieval era.

Some pilgrims had to cross bodies of water. Traveling by ship was not easy. The journey from Italy to the **Holy Land** could take more than six weeks. There was always the threat of shipwreck and pirates. Rats and fleas were abundant on these ships and the water on board was unhealthy. Pilgrims were packed into small boats and had barely enough room to roll over while they were sleeping.

To show people they were pilgrims, travelers wore a special uniform. This was a long robe, possibly blue, and a wide brimmed hat. The robe also acted as a sleeping bag of sorts. In addition, pilgrims used a metal-tipped **staff** for a walking stick. The staff could also be used as a weapon in case of attack. Pilgrims tied a soft leather bag, called a **scrip**, to their waist. They used this to hold all of their important belongings.

Like any travelers, pilgrims wanted souvenirs of their trip! The most popular souvenirs were badges. These badges proved that the pilgrim had made the difficult journey. Pilgrims wore their badges proudly on the brim of their

Words To Know

Holy Land: the land of ancient Palestine, important to Christian, Jewish, and Islamic religions.

staff: a straight walking stick.

scrip: a leather pouch.

ampuller: an artist who made and sold souvenirs to pilgrims.

prophet: a person who speaks for God.

croix: a French word meaning cross.

Allah: the Islamic term for God.

mosque: a Muslim house of worship.

hat or on their clothing. Scalloped shells were one of the first souvenirs that pilgrims could buy, and the scalloped shell became a symbol of a pilgrimage. Soon, though, other souvenirs were available. A group of artists known as **ampullers** sold badges, whistles, bells, and small bottles filled with holy water and what sellers claimed to be blood or fragments of a saint.

The Crusades

The city of Jerusalem is an important religious center. It had been the capital city of the Jewish people for hundreds of years. Then the Romans took over and Jerusalem became a Christian city in honor of Jesus Christ, who died there. But the Romans eventually lost control of the city to the Muslims. The Muslims believed that Jerusalem, which was the birthplace of the **prophet** Muhammad, was their holy land.

The Muslims allowed Christian pilgrims to worship in Jerusalem. But in 1071 a group of strict Muslims from central Asia captured the city. They said that Christians were no longer welcome there.

The Pope, who was the leader of the Catholic Church, called for a military expedition to free Jerusalem. This was called the First Crusade and it began in 1096. Christians who participated in the expedition cut crosses from red fabric and sewed them to their tunics. The French word *croix* means cross and the word evolved to *croisades*, or crusades.

DID YOU KNOW?

Churches competed with each other to attract pilgrims. They handed out pamphlets that listed the miracles that happened after people visited their holy relics. They composed songs and poems to entice people to visit. They also spent a lot of money decorating their reliquaries.

THE PROPHET MUHAMMAD

In the seventh century, an Arabian man named Muhammad began a new religion called Islam. Muhammad believed that God, called **Allah** in the Islamic faith, had spoken to him and told him that he was the most important prophet.

Muhammad preached the word of God. He fought with non-believing tribes and eventually united them under the banner of Islam. Today, Islam is one of the world's largest religions. People who practice the Islamic religion are called Muslims.

As the crusaders marched from different parts of Europe, thousands of men and women joined them. This was not a trained army—they had little knowledge of warfare or of what to expect. They traveled over land from France through modern-day Turkey. The conditions were harsh and the crusaders were ill-equipped. They marched for three and a half years! Many crusaders died along the way. Nevertheless, after a bloody battle, the crusaders succeeded in taking control of Jerusalem, again.

Many of the crusaders returned home. Those that remained in Jerusalem built castles, learned Arabic, and adopted the local style of dress. They mingled with the local population. They provided space in their churches for the Muslims to worship, and the Muslims built Christian chapels in their **mosques**. The people that lived in and around Jerusalem after the First Crusade got along very well in spite of their religious differences.

However, strict Muslims from Asia kept trying to take the city back. Sometimes they succeeded. Then another crusade would be launched from Europe. There were eight crusades in all, though none quite as passionate as the First Crusade. These later crusades were not very successful, either. The crusading Christians lost much of the land that they gained in the First Crusade, and despite their efforts, never regained control of Jerusalem.

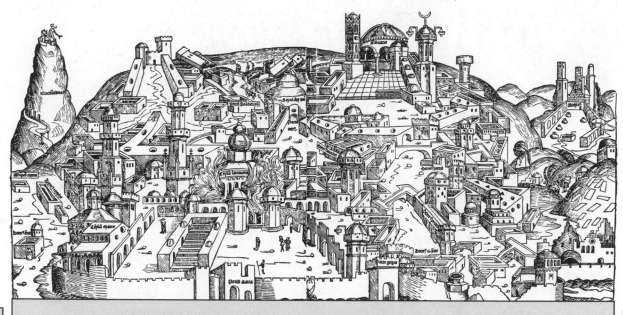

SAINT GEORGE AND THE DRAGON

In the early 300s, a Roman soldier named George proudly admitted that he was a Christian and refused to persecute other Christians as his commander ordered him to. For this, he was executed and eventually elevated to sainthood. Though Saint George died just as the medieval era began, he remained popular as a Christian hero throughout the Middle Ages.

Knights and crusaders brought home stories that they'd heard on their travels, and traveling bards collected stories to share. People loved to admire Saint George, and he became the focus of many fireside stories. One such story is that of Saint George and the Dragon. While Saint George never really faced a dragon, people liked to hear stories about bravery and honor.

According to the legend, a dragon made a nest at a spring that provided water for the city. In order to get water, the citizens had to figure out a way to move the dragon. Their solution was to offer a human sacrifice each day, with the victim determined by drawing lots. The day the beautiful princess was offered as a sacrifice, the people of the town were distraught, but no amount of pleading would save her. Just as the princess was about to meet her end, Saint George appeared to rescue her, slaying the dragon.

Some historians believe that the dragon represents a pagan cult, and the slaying of the dragon by Saint George represents the dominance of the Christian religion.

Make Your Own
Grail

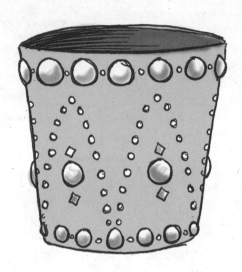

Supplies

gold or silver spray paint

a wooden dish of some sort, such as a tray, plate, or cup (you can often find these at garage sales)

glue

decorations such as flat marbles, beads, sequins, and glitter

1 Paint the dish with several coats of gold or silver—or both!

2 When the paint is dry, glue on whatever decorations you'd like. Try to create a dish worthy of a quest. Remember, you won't be able to use this for serving food or beverages, so you can make it as fancy as you'd like.

3 Once you've completed your grail, plan a real life quest by creating a treasure hunt for your friends.

DID YOU KNOW?
During the Middle Ages, leather drinking vessels were called jacks.

Make Your Own
Reliquary

Supplies

newspaper	an assortment of small trinkets such as buttons, beads, flat marbles, sequins, glitter
acrylic paint	
paint brush	
matchbox or other small cardboard box	all-purpose glue

1 Cover your work surface with newspaper. Paint the entire surface of the matchbox to cover the logos and words.

2 Paint the entire surface of the box with another coat of paint, such as gold or silver paint.

3 Once the top is dried, decorate the sides of the box with your small trinkets. Use your reliquary to store your special items.

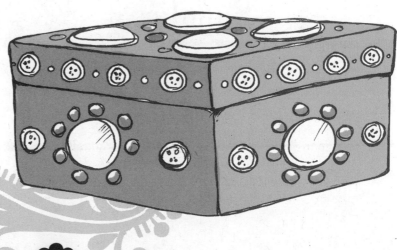

Make Your Own
Pilgrim's Badge

1 Mix cornstarch, baking soda, and water in a saucepan. With an adult's help, cook over medium heat until the mixture forms a clay-like consistency.

2 Dump the clay out onto the wooden cutting board or other work surface and allow it to cool a little bit. If you'd like, knead food coloring into the clay once it is cool enough to touch.

3 Break off a piece of clay and form it into the shape of a scallop shell, which was a common pilgrim's badge, or make a badge that represents a trip you've recently taken. Place the badge on a sheet of waxed paper to dry for several days.

4 Once the badge is thoroughly dried, glue the pin back to the back of the badge. When the glue is dry, wear your badge on a hat or put it on your backpack.

5 Wrap any leftover clay in a damp kitchen towel and store in a ziplock bag for another project.

Supplies

1 cup cornstarch

2 cups baking soda

1¼ cups water

saucepan

stove

wooden cutting board

food coloring (optional)

waxed paper

glue

pin back, available at craft stores

kitchen towel

ziplock bag

Monasteries **and** Monastic Life

As Christianity grew, religious institutions called **monasteries** became important in Western Europe. The people who lived in them were called **monks**. Monks had few possessions, ate simple food, and lived in very bare accommodations.

The monk's purpose was to achieve spiritual purity through a simple life in the monastery. Monks did physical labor and followed a daily routine of worship. They called this practice the **Divine Office**. Bells rang throughout the day to announce the hour so that the monks knew when to arrive for prayer or meals.

Large monasteries played a role in the community as well. The people who lived there practiced **almsgiving**, or what we might now call charity. The **almoner** shared food and clothing with the needy. Monasteries also provided shelter and food for travelers at a time when inns were hard to find.

An **abbot** ruled each monastery with absolute authority. The monks **revered** him. They bowed upon meeting the abbot and kissed his hands. If the abbot's name was mentioned in a letter as it was read aloud, the monks bowed toward him.

DID YOU KNOW?

Monks were only allowed to run if there was a fire or if a fellow monk was nearing death. Monks even had to keep their horse moving at a walk.

When a monk took his vows, he was bound to the monastery for life. Leaving the monastery required permission. So did speaking to anyone outside the monastery or even non-monks who worked within the monastery. In fact, monks could speak aloud only at certain times and in certain places. Because they passed so much of their lives in silence, the monks developed a sign language in order to communicate.

Monks wore a loose, sleeveless garment called a **habit**. The habit was ankle length and had a large hood that hid the monk's identity if he traveled through large towns.

The Monastery

When anyone older than fifteen joined the monastery, he became a **novice** for one year. It began with an initiation ceremony and mass where the novice's head was shaved, giving him the **tonsure**—the traditional haircut of a monk. During this year novices learned about life in a monastery and what was required of monks. Novices lived separately from the monks and were never permitted to be alone.

SIGN LANGUAGE FOR MONKS

- ✠ Bread: make a circle with both thumbs and index fingers, because bread was usually round.
- ✠ Fish: make swimming motions with your hand.
- ✠ A dish: hold your hand flat.

- ✠ Honey: stick your tongue out slightly and put your fingers on it (as if you were going to lick them).
- ✠ Vinegar: stroke your throat, because bitterness is tasted in the throat.

After the completion of his first year, a novice pledged himself to the monastic life. As part of the ceremony he received the traditional monk's cowl. For three days following his initiation he had to wear the cowl, sleep in his full habit, and refrain from speaking. On the third day, the priest of the week kissed him and pushed back his hood, and the new monk began his lifetime of days in the monastery.

For a time, some monasteries accepted children as young as five years old. These children were called **oblates**, meaning "offered ones." Oblates had several masters who kept them away from the monks, so that they would not be a disruption to the monastic life. The oblates were required to move in pairs. If one had to use the bathroom in the middle of the night, he woke his master who lit a lantern and woke a second boy to accompany them.

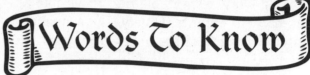

Words To Know

monastery: a religious house for monks.

monk: a religious man who lived a simple life to honor God.

Divine Office: a daily routine of worship.

almsgiving: giving food and other things to the poor.

almoner: a monk who shared food and clothing with the needy.

abbot: the person in charge of a monastery.

revere: to honor and show respect.

habit: the loose, sleeveless robe worn by monks.

novice: a man older than fifteen with one year's training to be a monk.

tonsure: the haircut style for monks. The top of their head was shaved, leaving a ring of hair from ear to ear.

oblates: children living in a monastery.

The oblates lived according to the monastic rules, although the monks gave them more food at mealtime and often an in—between meal snack (they must have realized that the boys were growing!). At mealtimes, an oblate ate at a table with the monks, but the monks did not allow him to sit. Instead, he stood across from a monk who was responsible for watching him, so the monk could report any misbehavior that required discipline.

The oblates learned to read, write, calculate, and speak Latin. They also practiced singing and reading music as this was necessary in order to participate in the Divine Office.

NUNS

Monasteries for women were called **nunneries**. Medieval women were severely limited in how they could live a respectable life: they could either marry or enter a nunnery. The nunneries recruited women from the upper classes. As a result, they often housed many women of high social standing.

Women could not become priests, but each nunnery did have an **abbess** (a female version of the abbot). When the nuns celebrated a mass, a male priest came to perform that service for them. Nuns wore their hair short and covered it with a veil. The veil symbolized marriage and showed that nuns were the brides of Christ.

Books

Monasteries played a large role in preserving written texts. Most of the books made during the Middle Ages were crafted by hand. Monks spent countless hours in the scriptorium copying texts, such as histories, plays, and even works by the famed medieval author Geoffrey Chaucer. Copying a text was very tedious, time-consuming work.

Manuscripts were copied onto **parchment**, which was made from sheep, goat, or calf hide. Before writing, the **scribe**, or writer, smoothed the parchment with **pumice** so that it would accept the ink. The scribe used a **quill** made from a swan or goose feather to write words. He dipped his quill in an inkpot. The main text was black ink. Once the main text was complete, he added the titles and headings in red. These were known as **rubrics**, from the Latin word *ruber*, for red.

GUTENBERG'S PRESS

Johannes Gutenberg usually gets credit for inventing the moveable type printing press in 1450 in Germany at the end of the Medieval era. There may have been other printing presses at the time, but Gutenberg's press was the best.

To print a page, the printer arranged the metal letters into the correct words inside a wooden frame. The type was set backward, since printing reverses the image. Then the printer tightened the frame, holding the letters in place, and applied ink to the letters. Finally, he put paper on top of the inked letters.

Before Gutenberg's press, books were a rarity and very expensive to own. Between the years 1450 and 1500, six thousand works were printed!

Words To Know

nunnery: monasteries for women.

abbess: the person in charge of a nunnery.

parchment: material for writing books, made from animal skin.

scribe: a man who copied books.

pumice: a type of rough stone.

quill: a writing tool made from a feather.

rubrics: titles and headings in a medieval book, written in red.

illuminated letter: the elaborate first letter drawn on each page of a medieval book.

The scribe left blank spaces allowing for illustrations that would come later. He also left out the first letter of each page. An artist would come back later and add in an **illuminated letter**. These letters were often detailed with lots of color and gold leaf. Medieval books were truly works of art.

Cathedrals and Churches

Words To Know

clergy: a priest, monk, or other person ordained by the church.

diocese: collection of parishes which a bishop is responsible for.

masons: craftsmen who built structures of stone.

flying buttresses: high arches on the outside of Gothic cathedrals. These supported the building's weight.

Monasteries were for monks, but cathedrals and churches were for ordinary people to worship in. Some churches were next to a monastery and served by the monks who lived there. But other churches were not affiliated with a monastery. A member of the **clergy** served these churches.

Many churches were scattered throughout the countryside and in towns and villages. Groups of churches in one large area combined to create a **diocese**, which a bishop ruled. Bishops held the highest position in the church. Cathedrals were the "mother church" of the diocese, and the church that the bishop considered his home. Cathedrals were huge, elaborate buildings complete with a throne for the bishop.

The architectural style of the late Middle Ages is called Gothic. Gothic cathedrals had grand arches and stained-glass windows that filled the inside of the church with colored light. Craftsmen called **masons** carved the stones that the cathedrals were built from. They developed a method of building that didn't require overly thick walls. Instead, they used **flying buttresses**, which helped carry the weight of the building. Notre Dame in Paris is one of the most famous cathedrals, but there are beautiful cathedrals all over Europe.

DID YOU KNOW?

Masons were paid for every stone they carved. Each mason cut a special mark into the stones he carved, so that he would receive pay for that stone.

Make Your Own
Sign Language

Supplies

pencil | paper

1 Make a list of the things you need to communicate to another person during the day. "Hello" and "Goodbye" are common and come with their own hand signal. But what about "What time is it" or "I'm going out to ride my bike"?

2 Once you have a list of the things you say frequently, devise a hand signal for each. Sketch a picture of the hand signal next to each communication so you don't forget.

3 Demonstrate the hand signals to the people you live with and then try to be completely silent for an hour or two, using only your hand signals. Not very easy, is it?

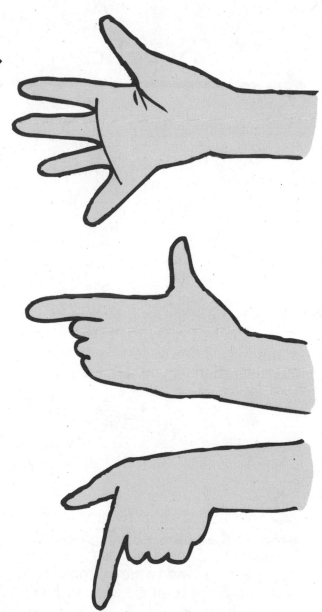

Make Your Own
Clay Pot Bell

Supplies

acrylic paints

paintbrush

clay pot

heavy twine,
24 inches long

two large
wooden beads

scissors

pencil

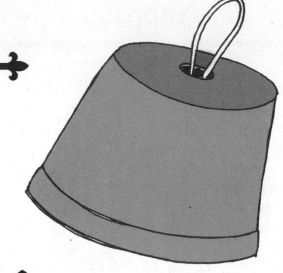

1 Paint a design on the clay pot. When the bell is finished the pot will hang upside down, so take that into consideration as you paint it.

2 Fold the piece of twine in half and tie a knot about 4 inches from the folded end. Slide a wooden bead over both ends of the twine all the way to the knot, and then tie another knot below the bead.

3 Push the loop into the clay pot and out the drain hole. Hang the bell from this loop. Trim off the extra length of twine.

4 To make a striker, glue the second wooden bead to one end of the pencil. Once dried, gently tap the bell with the strike. Try using your bell to call your family to dinner, just as the monks did.

Make Your Own
Illuminated Letter

Supplies

ruler

pencil

white cardstock

markers

glue

fine glitter or a metallic pen

newspaper

1 Measure and mark a 3-inch square onto the cardstock.

2 Inside the square, lightly sketch the first letter of your name so that it reaches the edge of the square. You can print or use cursive, or look at different fonts on your computer to get more ideas.

3 In the space surrounding the letter, sketch intricate designs like geometric patterns, vines, or squiggles.

4 Once you are happy with the design, use the markers to color the entire square, even the background.

5 Outline the letter (or other areas) with a thin line of glue and sprinkle on the fine glitter or use a metallic pen to add some sparkle. Shake the excess glitter off onto a sheet of newspaper so that you can pour it back into the glitter container.

6 If you like how this turned out, you can make enough letters to spell out your whole name.

Make Your Own
Stained Glass

1 Sketch a simple design on paper. Make sure that there is about 1 inch between each line; if the lines are too close together, you will have problems later. Once you are happy with how the design looks, use a marker to draw the lines darker.

2 Slide the paper with your design into the page protector.

3 Trace your design with a line of glue, making sure that all intersections meet. If the glue pulls away and leaves a gap in your line, don't try to fix it right away. Just let the outline dry and go back to fill in the missing parts of the line. Let your outlined pattern completely dry.

4 Mix different colors of food coloring into each of the remaining bottles of glue until the glue reaches the desired shade.

5 Carefully fill each section of the dried glue design, making sure that the colored glue completely touches all edges of each section. Continue

Supplies

pencil	several small containers of all-purpose glue
white paper	
marker	
clear plastic page protector	food coloring

in this manner, filling each section of the design. Again, don't try to fix gaps right away; once it's dry, go back and add more glue to fill in any gaps.

6 Once dried, peel your "stained glass" from the plastic page protector. You can press it onto a window to catch the light, just like the windows in cathedrals do.

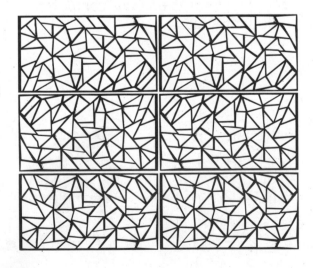

End *of an* Era

During the fifteenth century Europe began changing. Today we look back and call this time period that followed the Middle Ages the Renaissance, which means rebirth.

During this time there were great advances in science, and art became more valued. It was a gradual change, so the people who lived during this time didn't really realize they were stepping from one era to the next. Once the Renaissance era was in full swing, however, the more cultured people of that time period looked back at the medieval era with disdain.

Today, we have a more romantic notion of the Middle Ages, even if the lifestyle was simpler than we might imagine. Though the medieval era ended more than five hundred years ago, our world still shows reflections of the time period. The fascination we have with kings and queens and knights and castles is apparent in movies, books, and games.

The stories of Robin Hood and King Arthur have been made into numerous movies, but there are other movies that feature a touch of the Middle Ages. The *Princess Bride*, *Monty Python and the Holy Grail*, and even *Shrek* entertain us with a Medieval touch.

Fans of the Harry Potter series will recognize many medieval elements in those popular books. Hogwarts School of Witchcraft and Wizardry is housed in a castle and the school robes resemble some of the flowing garments that were popular during the Middle Ages. And of course magic, wizards, and dragons have deep roots in the medieval era. In the *Lord of the Rings*, characters battle with medieval-style weaponry and wear clothing reminiscent of the Middle Ages.

The popular role-playing game, Dungeons and Dragons, features medieval characters and mythical creatures straight out of the Middle Ages. Warhammer, a game that's played both live and online takes its name from a medieval weapon that was used in hand-to-hand combat. While Warhammer is a fantasy game played in a fictional universe, there's no denying that it features some medieval elements as wizards and kings battle a plague. Even the classic game of chess— developed at the end of the medieval era—features playing pieces that represent important medieval characters.

Some people are so entranced with the Middle Ages and the Renaissance that they actually time travel. Well, almost! Costumed as peasants and nobles, medievalists and re-enactors visit large festivals that are committed to bringing that period to life. These festivals offer people the chance to try their hand at dressing in the style of the Middle Ages, speaking Old English, and watching mounted competitors joust in the old tradition. These fairs are open to the public, and anyone wishing to get a sense of the medieval era can attend.

abbess: the person in charge of a nunnery.

abbot: the person in charge of a monastery.

accolade: an open-handed blow to the neck or head, or a light sword touch to the shoulder.

alchemy: a medieval chemical science that tried to change regular metal into gold, discover a universal cure for disease, and prolong life forever.

Allah: the Islamic term for God.

alliance: an agreement between two parties.

almoner: a monk who shared food and clothing with the needy.

alms: giving money or food to the poor.

ampuller: an artist who made and sold souvenirs to pilgrims.

anarchy: a society without a strong government.

Anglo-Saxons: the people from Germanic tribes who migrated to the island of Britain.

apothecary: a medieval pharmacist.

Arabians: people from the Arabian Peninsula.

arrow loop: a narrow vertical slit in the castle wall that soldiers fired arrows through.

aristocracy: nobility, or a hereditary ruling class.

awl: a small, pointed tool.

barbarians: people that the Romans thought were primitive.

bard: a traveling musician.

baron: the lowest grade of nobility. A baron held land that had been granted him by the king.

battering ram: a covered structure with a large, horizontal log hanging from it that soldiers repeatedly swung against a castle's wall or door.

battle-ax: a weapon with a metal blade attached to a wooden handle.

bedchamber: the sleeping area.

bishop: an important person in the church having authority over priests.

Black Death: an infectious disease.

breach: to get through a fortification.

brewhouse: a building where servants made ale.

brocade: fabric woven with elaborate designs.

bubonic plague: infectious disease carried by rats and mice that spread to humans.

buttery: a room where wine and ale was stored.

byre: a barn.

Byzantine Empire: a nineteenth century term used to describe what was left of the Roman Empire during the Middle Ages.

cadency mark: a symbol to indicate a knight's place within his family.

caltrops: sharp, pointed iron objects that could lame a horse.

caravan: a large group of people traveling together.

cathedral: the church that contains the throne, or official seat, of the bishop of the diocese and therefore the "mother church" of the diocese.

cavalry: soldiers on horseback.

census: an inventory that tells the king about every person and animal in the kingdom.

cesspit: a hole in the ground for waste.

chandler: a tradesman who made candles.

charter: a document that protects the king's subjects from unfair actions.

chausses: mail to protect the legs.

chivalry: a knight's code of conduct.

clergy: a priest, monk, or other person ordained by the church.

cloister: the common area of a monastery.

coat of arms: the colors, patterns, and symbols on a shield.

cobbles: fist-sized round stones used to pave roads.

commerce: an exchange of goods.

communes: cities that governed themselves.

coppicing: a method for harvesting wood that allowed the tree to continue growing.

count: man assigned by the king to oversee and manage property.

court: a group who helped and supported the king and queen.

court jester: the court's official entertainer.

cowl: the loose, sleeveless robe worn by monks.

croft: a peasant's plot of land.

croix: a French word meaning cross.

Crown Prince: the king's first-born son, who inherits the throne.

crucifixion: the death of Jesus Christ upon the cross.

curfew: the time when people are required to be in their homes.

curtain walls: the outer walls of a castle complex.

curtsy: a respectful gesture made by women, requiring them to bend their knees and lower their body.

dagger: a small knife used in hand-to-hand combat.

dais: a raised area at the back of the hall where a baron's family and guests dined.

diocese: collection of parishes overseen by a bishop.

Glossary

Divine Office: a daily routine of worship.

dormitory: a large room where monks slept.

dubbing: the act of making a squire a knight.

fast days: days designated by the church that had special eating requirements.

famine: a shortage of food.

fief: the land given to a baron or vassal.

feudal lord: a member of feudal society who owned land and had power over others.

feudal society: the social system that developed in Europe between the ninth and fifteenth centuries. Kings and barons provided land to vassals in exchange for their loyalty.

firepot: clay pot filled with a flaming liquid like tar used to attack a castle during a siege.

flail: a weapon with an iron ball attached to a wooden handle with a length of chain.

flying buttresses: high arches on the outside of Gothic cathedrals that support the building's weight.

fortification: walled-in area to protect against an enemy.

Franks: people of German descent.

garderobe: the bathroom facility in a castle.

garrison: a group of soldiers ready to protect an area.

gatehouse: a structure built at the entrance to the monastery or a castle.

gomphus: a curved stick used for cleaning oneself in the bathroom.

Great Hall: a large living and dining area where the nobles held court, managed business, entertained, and ate.

Greek fire: a flammable material used in warfare.

guild: an organization established to protect merchants.

hauberk: a thigh-length mail shirt with elbow-length sleeves.

hearth: an open fireplace in the center of a house.

heir: a person who inherits a title or property from a parent.

hennin: a tall hat worn by ladies

heraldry: the practice of decorating shields.

heresy: having a belief that is not approved of by the church.

heretic: someone who speaks out against the church.

Holy Grail: the mythical vessel used by Jesus.

Holy Land: the land of ancient Palestine, important to Christian, Jewish, and Islamic religions.

holy relics: items that the Christian people considered sacred.

hostel: an overnight facility.

Huns: nomads from central Asia.

illuminated letter: the elaborate first letter drawn on each page of a medieval book.

jacks: leather drinking vessels.

jury system: a court of law in which a jury, or group of citizens, decides whether the accused is innocent or guilty.

keep: the primary living area of the castle.

kings: male rulers with supreme power or authority over their land.

knights: men who fought for and protected the lands of their lord, baron, count, or king.

lance: a long, straight wooden spear.

legend: an ancient story that may or may not have happened.

Lent: a season of fasting for the forty days before Easter.

leper: person infected with leprosy.

lord: a noble who owned or managed the manor.

lunellum: a tool used for scraping parchment.

manor: land granted to a baron by the king.

masons: craftsmen who built structures of stone.

mead: a sweet alcoholic drink.

medieval Europe: Europe during the Middle Ages, a period of time from about 350 to 1450 CE.

midwife: a woman skilled in helping birth babies.

miller: a man who ground grain into flour for bread.

monarch: a supreme head of state, such as a king or queen.

monarchy: the kind of government ruled by a monarch.

monastery: a religious house for monks.

monk: a religious man who lived a simple life to honor God.

mosque: a Muslim house of worship.

myth: a traditional story dealing with ancestors or heroes, or even supernatural figures.

Normans: people from medieval northern France, with Scandinavian roots.

Normandy: a region in northern France.

novice: a man older than fifteen with one year's training to be a monk.

nunnery: monasteries for women.

oblates: children living in a monastery.

opiates: drugs used as pain relievers.

oubliette: an underground dungeon.

pagan: a non-Christian who worshipped the natural world and many different gods.

page: a boy who acted as a knight's apprentice.

Glossary

palisades: curtain walls made of timber that were common in the early Middle Ages.

pallet: a cushioned sleeping surface.

parchment: material for writing books, made from animal skin.

parishes: a division of land that had its own church.

peasant: a farmer in feudal society who lived on and farmed land owned by his lord.

penance: punishment dictated by the church.

pilgrim: a person making a pilgrimage.

pilgrimage: a trip to visit a holy relic or sacred place.

plague: an infectious disease.

pokerounce: toast spread with honey and pine nuts.

Pope: the head of the Roman Catholic church.

potage: a type of vegetable soup.

privy: a small toilet structure, separate from the house.

prophet: a person who speaks for God.

pumice: a type of rough stone.

quill: a writing tool made from a feather

quintain: a dummy suspended from a swinging pole used by knights in practice.

raiders: men who stole from churches and the homes of the wealthy.

ration: limiting the amount of food and water used each day.

reign: the period of time that a king rules.

reliquary: a fancy container used to hold holy relics.

revere: to honor and show respect.

rubrics: titles and headings written in red.

rushlights: lamps made of rushes, or cattails.

sacred: highly valued and important.

Saxons: a group of old Germanic tribes descending from northern Germany and the eastern Netherlands.

scabbard: a sheath that holds a sword.

scribe: a man who copied books.

scrip: a leather pouch.

scriptorium: area in a monastery where books and documents were written, copied, and illuminated.

scullion: a person who washed and cleaned the kitchen.

secular: not affiliated with a monastery.

serf: a member of the lowest feudal class in medieval Europe.

shaffron: a piece of armor meant to protect a horse's head.

Shrove Tuesday: the day before the Christian season of Lent.

siege: surrounding a fortification.

siege tower: a giant wooden structure that attacking armies used to breach castle walls.

sinner: a person that does wrong according to the church.

squire: a young man of fourteen who successfully finished his training as a page.

staff: a straight walking stick.

statutes: rules.

sumptuary laws: laws requiring each social class to dress within certain guidelines.

surnames: last names.

tapestries: colorful, woven fabric hanging that often portrayed a scene from daily life or mythology.

tenant: someone who pays rent to use land or buildings owned by someone else.

thatched roof: a roof made of dried plant materials such as reeds, straw, and heather.

tincture: the background, or field, of a shield.

tithes: a portion of each household's animals and crops paid to the church.

tonsure: the haircut style for monks. The top of their head was shaved, leaving a ring of hair from ear to ear.

torche-culs: handfuls of straw or hay used for cleaning oneself in the bathroom.

tournament: a competition where knights used their lances to try to knock an opponent off his horse.

tradesmen: a skilled worker, such as a stonecutter.

trebuchet: a large, catapult-like structure with a moveable arm that launched damaging items into or over castle walls.

trencher: a piece of stale bread used as a plate.

truckle bed: a small bed that slid under a larger bed.

usurers: moneylenders who charged interest on their loans.

vamplate: a round disk of iron mounted to a lance that protected the knight's arm and hand.

vassal: a knight who also farmed his fief.

Vikings: people from the northern lands of what is now Denmark, Norway, Sweden, and Finland.

villeins: with respect to their lord, villeins were serfs, but they were free men in dealing with other people.

wattle and daub: a building method using small branches and vines (the wattle) and a mixture of clay, dung, and straw (the daub) to hold the branches together.

whetstone: a stone for sharpening knives.

wimple: a head cover worn by women.

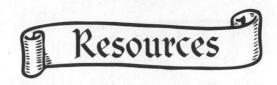

Resources

BOOKS

Bishop, Morris. *The Middle Ages*. New York, NY: First Mariner Books, 2001.

Blackwood, Bary L. *Life in a Medieval Castle*. San Diego, CA: Lucent Books, 2000.

Butt, John J. *Daily Life in the age of Charlemagne*. Westport, CT: Greenwood Press, 2002

Corrick, James A. *Life of a Medieval Knight*. San Diego, CA: Lucent Books, 2001.

Haywood, John. *Atlas of Past Times*. Ann Arbor, MI: Borders Press, 2003.

Gravett, Christopher. *Eyewitness Knight*. New York, NY: DK Publishing Inc., 2007.

Rowling, Marjorie. *Everyday Life in Medieval Times*. New York, NY: G.P. Putnam's Sons, 1969.

Sancha, Sheila. *The Luttrell Village: Country Life in the Middle Ages*. New York, NY: Thomas Y. Crowell, 1983.

Singman, Jeffrey L. *Daily Life in Medieval Europe*. Westport, CT: Greenwood Press, 1999.

Slater, Stephen. *The Complete Book of Heraldry*. London: Hermes House, 2003.

WEB SITES

www.encarta.msn.com

www.fitzmuseum.cam.ac.uk/pharos/sections/making_art/index_manuscript.html

www.bayeuxtapestry.org.uk/ **Reading Museum Service**

www.bl.uk/treasures/magnacarta/basics.html **The British Library**

www.ucalgary.ca/UofC/eduweb/engl401/ **University of Calgary**

www.historyforkids.org/

www.kitchenproject.com/history/Pretzel.htm

www.castles-of-britain.com/castle32.htm

www.gale.cengage.com **Gale Virtual Reference Library**

www.the-orb.net **The online reference book for medieval studies**

www.history.uk.com/articles/index.php?archive=44

www.courses.fas.harvard.edu/~chaucer/special/lifemann/manners/urbanit.html

www.pbs.org/wgbh/nova/lostempires/trebuchet/race.html

www.library.nd.edu/rarebooks/digital_projects/heraldry/cadency.shtml

www.fleurdelis.com/meanings.htm

http://scholar.chem.nyu.edu/tekpages/Technology.html

www.dartfordarchive.org.uk/medieval/people_lep.shtml

www.stjoan-center.com

www.intermaggie.com/med/humors.php

www.encyclopedia.com/doc/1G1-55343375.html

www.collectionscanada.ca/eppp-archive/100/201/300/cdn_medical_association/cmaj/vol-159/issue-12/1482.htm

www.newadvent.org/cathen/06719a.htm

www.unrv.com/empire/roman-population.php

www.medievalcrusades.com/crusadesbegin.htm

www.pbs.org/wgbh/masterpiece/merchant/ei_shylock.html

Index

Index

K

keeps, 50, 54
kings, 10, 12, 15–20, 50
kitchens, 60, 68
knights, 8–9, 11–13, 24–41, 96
Knights Templar, 33–34
knives, 30, 68

L

lances, 28–29, 30, 32
languages, 9, 14, 18, 106, 107, 111
legends, 2, 8–9, 34, 93, 101, 116
leprosy/lepers, 82, 90
lords, 1, 2, 12, 26–27, 60

M

magic/magicians, 93, 94, 116
Magna Carta, 19
mail, 29, 30–31, 38–39
manners, 60, 61
map, 5
markets, 86
marriages, 16, 18, 71–73, 89, 108
medicine, 22, 82–83
medieval era, 1–3
merchants, 22, 34, 86, 97. *See also* tradesmen
Middle Ages, 3, 5
military religious orders, 33–34
monarchy, 15, 16
monasteries/monks, 105–110

money, 34, 53, 70, 92
Muhammad (the prophet), 99, 100
Muslims, 99–100

N

names, 11, 17
nobles/nobility, 12, 14, 15–20, 25, 27–28, 50–51, 57, 60, 69, 71–73, 78
Normans/Norman conquest, 4, 17, 18, 51
nunneries/nuns, 108

P

pagans/paganism, 92–93, 101
pages, 25–26
patron saints, 94–95
peasants, 1, 2, 11, 12, 14, 33, 53, 66–73
pilgrims/pilgrimages, 96–99, 104
plague, 81–82
Pope, the, 16, 34, 92, 94, 99
princes/princesses, 16–18

Q

queens, 15–20, 50
quintain, 30

R

relics/reliquaries, 96, 99, 103
religion, 2, 13, 27–28, 33–34, 73, 89, 91–101, 105. *See also* Church, the

Renaissance, 3, 115–116
Richard the Lionheart, 18, 19, 34
Robin Hood, 34, 116
Roman Empire, 3, 6–7, 9, 10, 11

S

saints, 94–95
serfs, 11, 12
shields, 35–37
sickness, 22, 81–83
siege weapons, 43–48
sieges, 43–48, 52–55, 57
sign language, 106, 107, 111
Silk Road, 22, 97
soldiers. *See* armies; knights
squires, 26–28, 30
storytelling, 20, 51, 101
swords, 9, 26, 28–29, 57

T

tapestries, 50–51, 58
torture, 34, 56–57, 92
tournaments, 31–32
Tower of London, 56
tradesmen, 1, 2, 83–85. *See also* merchants

travel, 20, 22, 36, 86, 96–100, 106
trebuchets, 44, 45, 46–47
trenchers, 61, 62
tunnels, 45, 54

V

vassals, 11–13
villages, 1, 65–73

W

walls, 42–45, 50, 53–54, 79
war/warfare, 7, 13, 17, 24, 42–48, 49, 99–100. *See also* armies; Crusades
water, 52, 56, 68, 69, 80, 98
weapons, 24–26, 28–33, 43–48, 53, 57, 116
William the Conqueror, 17, 56
witchcraft, 93–94, 116
women, 70–73, 82, 108